DIPS & SPREADS

DIPS & SPREADS

46 Gorgeous & Good-for-You Recipes

Dawn Yanagihara

Photographs by Angie Cao

CHRONICLE BOOKS

SAN FRANCISCO

Text copyright © 2015 by Dawn Yanagihara.
Photographs copyright © 2015 by Angie Cao.

Library of Congress Cataloging-in-Publication Data:

Yanagihara, Dawn.

Dips & spreads : 46 gorgeous & good-for-you recipes / Dawn Yanagihara.

   pages cm

Includes index.

ISBN 978-1-4521-4908-0

1. Dips (Appetizers) I. Title. II. Title: Dips and spreads.

TX740.Y35 2015

641.81'2—dc23

                    2015008238

Manufactured in China

MIX
Paper from
responsible sources
FSC
www.fsc.org   FSC™ C008047

Designed by Alice Chau

Food styling by Fanny Pan

Chronicle books and gifts are available at special quantity discounts to corporations, professional associations, literacy programs, and other organizations. For details and discount information, please contact our premiums department at corporatesales@chroniclebooks.com or at 1-800-759-0190.

10 9 8 7 6 5 4 3 2 1

Chronicle Books LLC
680 Second Street
San Francisco, California 94107
www.chroniclebooks.com

CONTENTS

VEGETABLES & HERBS

OLIVES, NUTS & SEEDS

YOGURT & CHEESE

SALT & SEA

INTRODUCTION

Here's a truth: Everyone loves a good dip. This is true for a few reasons. For one, eating with our hands is supremely gratifying. There are no dinner-table formalities, or even utensils, to detract from the pleasures of eating delicious food. Then there's the social act of dipping into a communal bowl, and our natural association of dips with parties. Dips are not weeknight fare. Rather, they make appearances—along with libations, usually—at informal gatherings and celebrations, so how can we not equate a dip with merriment? Finally, the "serve yourself" approach to dips means customized noshing. With no preset or plated portions set in front of us, we choose for ourselves the item to dunk (pita chip or carrot stick?), scoop up as little or as much as we want (fearful of or intrepid about garlic breath?), and repeat as many times as we like (just three bites or do we quietly polish off the bowl?).

The dips that most of us grew up eating are decidedly retro. They're laden with mayonnaise, bogged down by cream cheese, and seasoned with soup packets. They tasted good then, and we still like them, but a large part of their appeal is in the nostalgia they evoke. If you're like me, these days you prefer foods that satisfy because they're wholesome and they derive their taste from fresh, robustly flavored ingredients, not from a surfeit of unhealthful or fatty processed products. (The exception: bacon, which sneaked its way into just one recipe in this collection.)

Fortunately, the cuisines of the Mediterranean, Middle East, and South Asia include myriad dips and spreads—from chunky, rustic tapenade to smooth, spreadable hummus. Ingredients such as legumes, pulses, vegetables, nuts, olives, or yogurt are used as a base, and aromatic spices, fragrant herbs, pungent garlic, or fruity olive oil serve as flavorings. Some of the dips and spreads that you'll find in these pages are traditional, time-tested combinations; some are riffs on classics; and some are original creations. Many are vegan, most are vegetarian, and quite a few can be made with less effort than you probably thought possible. All are flavor-packed and healthful, so you can dip and spread with abandon.

TIPS FOR DELIGHTFUL DIPS AND SUPERB SPREADS

As far as dishes for entertaining go, dips and spreads are by far the easiest to make. And since most achieve peak taste only after the ingredients have had the opportunity to mingle for at least 30 minutes, there's no need for last-minute preparations or carefully orchestrated timing. For optimal flavor, here are a few dip and spread tips to bear in mind.

GET RID OF (GARLIC) GERMS

Although garlic is available year-round in grocery stores, it does have a season (summer). Garlic that has been stored for out-of-season use has thick, papery outer layers, and the cloves often contain germs, or green shoots, which at later stages of development sprout from the tops of the cloves. The germ, when raw, tastes acrid and hot. When a recipe calls for raw garlic—and lots of recipes in this book do—it's best to check whether there's a germ at the center of the clove and, if there is, to remove it before chopping or mincing. To do this, simply halve the clove lengthwise, look for a green core in each half and, if present, use the tip of a paring knife to pry it out. (A very young germ may be pale yellow in color and not so sharp in flavor, but you may as well remove it since you've opened the clove.) Cooking tames the harsh flavor of the germ, so removal isn't necessary for garlic that sees heat. Please note that these recipes specify the size of garlic cloves to be used. This is important because when you're making just a bowl or so, as these recipes do, the amount of garlic used has to be carefully balanced with the other ingredients.

'TIS THE SEASON(ING)

Don't be timid when seasoning a dip with salt and pepper. When I taste a dip after making it and think it's missing something, more salt is often the answer. A squeeze of lemon juice or a splash of another acidic ingredient (such as wine vinegar) also enhances flavors. Tasted on its own, a properly seasoned dip should verge on overseasoned. Keep in mind that the amount of dip scooped up on a dipper is usually quite small and the dipper itself is relatively mild, so the dip needs to be flavor-packed. (That said, if you're serving extremely salty crackers or chips, don't be overzealous when seasoning your dip.)

TEMPER, TEMPER

Cold temperature dulls flavors in foods of all sorts, and it stiffens consistencies, too. For these reasons, it's best to give any dip or spread that's been refrigerated a chance to lose its chill before serving (an exception is Roasted Red Pepper and Chipotle Whipped Feta on page 94, which has the best consistency when it is slightly chilled). Allow the dip 45 to 60 minutes at room temperature and give it a stir or two during that time to help it along.

THE LAST WORD: GARNISH

Many dips and spreads benefit from a garnish—a smattering of herbs, a sprinkle of nuts, a dusting of spice, a drizzle of extra-virgin olive oil. Olive oil adds an attractive glisten and helps prevent the surface of the dip from drying out. It also supplies its own nuances (fruity, peppery, buttery) and, as a fat, carries the flavors of the other ingredients, so that the dip tastes richer, deeper, and more complex. If you've made your dip several hours in advance, chop the herb garnish right before using. And no matter what types of garnishes you're using, add them just before serving so they look fresh and vibrant.

WHAT TO SERVE WITH?

For dips and spreads with thick, dense, or firm consistencies, offer dippers with enough substance and structure, such as toasted baguette slices or carrot crudités, so that they won't snap or break during scooping or slathering. Thin, more fluid dips are usually best served with absorbent items, such as slices of fresh baguette, fresh pita bread, and focaccia or vegetables with textures that can grip or shapes that can scoop. Dips that fall in the middle in consistency work with dippers of all sorts. Each recipe in this book offers basic suggestions for what to dip. Following are possibilities in greater detail, with brief instructions for preparing them.

BABY ARTICHOKES / Remove tough outer leaves, peel the stems, and trim the tops. Cut the artichokes into halves or quarters, toss with a good amount of olive oil and salt and pepper, and roast on a baking sheet in a 400°F [200°C] oven until browned and tender, 15 to 20 minutes, stirring once about halfway through. (Don't overcook, which can make the artichokes too soft and delicate for dipping.)

CHIPS / Chips offer crunchy texture and sturdy structure. Corn, rice, veggie, bagel, pita, and multigrain are just some of the options out there. Pita chips are especially versatile—sturdy yet slightly absorbent, they work well with almost any type of dip. If you're serving chips with assertively fla-vored dips and spreads, make sure they're a good match. For example, cheddar-flavored chips would be an utter mismatch for a goat-cheese dip.

CRACKERS / Plain, neutral-tasting crack-ers that are not too salty work well with most types of dips and spreads. Seeded and whole-grain crackers are quite versa-tile, too—their subtle nuttiness comple-ments dips and spreads with sweet, fruity, or earthy flavors. Assertively seasoned crackers, for example onion or caraway, may be overpowering and require careful matching.

CRUDITÉS / Some veggies, such as car-rots, celery, sweet peppers, cucumbers, cherry tomatoes, radishes (ideally with their tops attached), endive leaves, and jicama, are best raw. Others, such as asparagus, broccoli, cauliflower, and snap peas, are best lightly blanched. To blanch, bring a large pot of salted water to a boil, drop in the veggies, and cook just until crisp-tender, generally no more than a minute or two. Don't overcook, which will result in soft, limp dippers. Drain the veggies and immediately drop them into a large bowl filled with ice water to stop the cooking and set their color. As soon as they're cool, drain again and pat dry; don't leave them languishing in the ice-water bath, lest they become waterlogged.

FOCACCIA / Cut the loaf into cubes or short, easy-to-dip sticks.

FRESH BAGUETTE SLICES / This is an easy, dependable, and always solid option, but slices of fresh baguette (or similar bread) should be consumed quickly or replenished frequently because they dry out within 30 minutes or so of cutting. Serving the slices, covered, in a bowl or basket lined with a fabric napkin or clean kitchen towel will help keep them fresh.

GRISSINI (A.K.A. ITALIAN BREAD STICKS) / Grissini have a great shape (long and slender) and appealing texture (super-crunchy). Standing them vertically in a glass for serving makes them visually interesting and easy to grasp.

PITA BREAD, LAVASH, AND NAAN / Cut pita rounds into wedges, and lavash and naan into manageable pieces. If possible, serve these flatbreads covered with a napkin or kitchen towel to prevent them from drying out too quickly.

ROASTED POTATOES / At room temperature, the texture of roasted potatoes tends to be rather dense and firm, so roasted spuds are best with dips or spreads that are lithe, creamy, and not too starchy or heavy. Choose red or Yukon gold potatoes that measure about 1½ in [4 cm] in diameter. Cut each spud into quarters (or halves, if the potatoes are small—the pieces should be close to bite-size), toss with a generous amount of olive oil, and season with salt and pepper. Distribute the potatoes in a single layer on a rimmed baking sheet, making sure that they are not crowded (which would impede browning), and roast in a 450°F [230°C] oven for 25 to 30 minutes. Halfway through roasting, use a metal spatula to carefully scrape along the bottom of the baking sheet to loosen the potatoes and stir. Once they're out of the oven, roasted potatoes are best served within a few hours.

TOASTED BAGUETTE SLICES (A.K.A. CROSTINI) / Brush slices with oil, sprinkle with salt and pepper, and brown under a broiler or in a hot oven. For a mild garlic flavor, rub the toasted slices with a smashed garlic clove. Toasted baguette slices won't go stale as quickly as fresh.

LEGUMES
&
PULSES

Creamy, earthy, slightly nutty, a touch tangy

MAKES / about 1½ cups [370 g]

SERVE WITH / Crackers, crudités, pita bread, pita chips

STORAGE / Can be refrigerated without garnish for up to 5 days; bring to room temperature, stir to recombine, and garnish before serving

CLASSIC HUMMUS

One 15-oz [425-g] can chickpeas, rinsed and drained

¼ cup [60 g] tahini

1 medium garlic clove, germ removed (see page 9), chopped

¼ tsp ground cumin

Fine sea salt

3½ Tbsp freshly squeezed lemon juice

1 Tbsp water

3 Tbsp extra-virgin olive oil, plus more for drizzling

Paprika, ground sumac, or chopped fresh flat-leaf parsley leaves for garnish

Set aside 16 or so whole chickpeas for garnish.

In a food processor, combine the remaining chickpeas, the tahini, garlic, cumin, and ½ tsp salt. Pulse about ten times, until the chickpeas are coarsely chopped. With the machine running, stream in the lemon juice and water and process to a thick, relatively smooth purée, 1 to 1½ minutes, scraping down the bowl once or twice. With the machine running, stream in the olive oil and continue to process until the mixture is as smooth as it can be, about 1 minute, scraping down the bowl once or twice. Taste and adjust the seasoning with more salt, if needed.

Transfer the hummus to a wide, shallow bowl for serving. Cover and let stand at room temperature for about 30 minutes to allow the flavors to meld.

Use the back of a spoon to swirl the surface of the dip. Sprinkle with paprika, scatter the reserved whole chickpeas over the top, drizzle with olive oil, and serve.

NOTE / *This recipe can be doubled if you're serving a large crowd or you like to keep extra hummus on hand.*

Spicy, earthy, subtly sweet, a touch nutty

MAKES / about 2 cups [460 g]

SERVE WITH / Crackers, crudités, pita bread, pita chips

STORAGE / Can be refrigerated without garnish for up to 5 days; bring to room temperature, stir to recombine, and garnish before serving

ROASTED RED PEPPER HUMMUS
WITH HARISSA

One 15-oz [425-g] can chickpeas, rinsed and drained

½ cup [100 g] drained jarred roasted red peppers, patted dry

1 large garlic clove, germ removed (see page 9), chopped

2½ Tbsp freshly squeezed lemon juice

2 Tbsp tahini

1½ tsp harissa, plus more to taste

½ tsp smoked paprika

Pinch of ground cumin

Fine sea salt

3 Tbsp extra-virgin olive oil, plus more for drizzling

In a food processor, combine the chickpeas, red peppers, garlic, lemon juice, tahini, harissa, smoked paprika, cumin, and 1 tsp salt. Pulse about ten times, until the chickpeas and peppers are coarsely chopped. Scrape down the bowl and process to a thick purée, about 10 seconds. Scrape down the bowl once again. With the machine running, stream in the olive oil and continue to process until the mixture is as smooth as it can be, about 1 minute, scraping down the bowl once or twice. Taste and adjust the seasoning with more salt and harissa, if needed.

Transfer the hummus to a wide, shallow bowl for serving. Cover and let stand at room temperature for about 30 minutes to allow the flavors to meld.

Use the back of a spoon to swirl the surface of the dip. Drizzle with olive oil and serve.

Smooth, earthy, sweet, nutty, slightly smoky

MAKES / about 2½ cups [610 g]

SERVE WITH / Crackers, crudités, pita bread, pita chips

STORAGE / Can be refrigerated without garnish for up to 5 days; bring to room temperature, stir to recombine, and garnish before serving

SWEET POTATO HUMMUS
WITH SMOKED PAPRIKA

One 8-oz [230-g] orange-fleshed sweet potato, scrubbed

2 medium garlic cloves, unpeeled, woody ends trimmed

One 15-oz [425-g] can chickpeas, rinsed and drained

3 Tbsp tahini

3 Tbsp freshly squeezed lemon juice

1 Tbsp water

¾ tsp smoked paprika, plus more for garnish

⅜ tsp ground cumin

Fine sea salt

¼ cup [60 ml] extra-virgin olive oil, plus more for drizzling

Preheat the oven to 375°F [190°C]. Line a small baking sheet with aluminum foil.

Pierce the sweet potato a few times with the tip of a paring knife and set it on the prepared baking sheet. Drop the garlic cloves onto the baking sheet. Roast for 15 minutes, then remove the garlic cloves and set aside. Continue to roast the sweet potato until a skewer inserted into the thickest part meets no resistance, about 1 hour. Let cool completely on the baking sheet.

Peel the garlic cloves and the sweet potato. Cut the sweet potato into largish chunks.

In a food processor, combine the chickpeas, sweet potato chunks, roasted garlic, tahini, lemon juice, water, smoked paprika, cumin, and 1 tsp salt. Pulse about ten times, until the chickpeas are coarsely chopped. Scrape down the bowl and process to a thick purée, about 1 minute. Scrape down the bowl once again. With the machine running, stream in the olive oil and continue to process until the mixture is as smooth as it can be, about 1 minute, scraping down the bowl once or twice. Taste and adjust the seasoning with more salt, if needed.

CONTINUED

Transfer the hummus to a wide, shallow bowl for serving. Cover and let stand at room temperature for about 30 minutes to allow the flavors to meld.

Use the back of a spoon to swirl the surface of the dip. Drizzle with olive oil, sprinkle with smoked paprika, and serve.

MAKES / about 2½ cups [600 g]

SERVE WITH / Crackers, crudités, fresh or toasted baguette slices, grissini, pita chips, roasted potato wedges

STORAGE / Best served the day it's made, but can be refrigerated without garnish for up to 2 days (color will dull with storage); bring to room temperature, stir to recombine, and garnish before serving

WHITE BEAN DIP
WITH ARUGULA AND ANCHOVIES

Two 15-oz [425-g] cans cannellini beans, rinsed and drained

2 cups [30 g] lightly packed baby arugula, plus torn leaves for garnish

2 large oil-packed anchovy fillets, roughly chopped

1 large garlic clove, germ removed (see page 9), chopped

1½ Tbsp freshly squeezed lemon juice

Fine sea salt and freshly ground black pepper

¼ cup [60 ml] extra-virgin olive oil, plus more for drizzling

In a food processor, combine the beans, arugula, anchovies, garlic, lemon juice, ½ tsp salt, and ¼ tsp pepper. Process to a thick purée, 45 to 60 seconds, scraping down the bowl once or twice. With the machine running, stream in the olive oil and continue to process until the mixture is smooth and creamy, about 30 seconds. Taste and adjust the seasoning with salt and pepper, if needed.

Transfer the dip to a wide, shallow bowl for serving. Cover and let stand at room temperature for about 30 minutes to allow the flavors to meld.

Use the back of a spoon to swirl the surface of the dip. Garnish with arugula leaves, drizzle with olive oil, and serve.

Creamy, fragrant, super garlicky (roasted, not raw, garlic), herbaceous

MAKES / about 2½ cups [600 g]

SERVE WITH / Crackers, crudités, fresh or toasted baguette slices, grissini

STORAGE / Can be refrigerated without garnish for up to 2 days (garlic flavor will intensify with storage); bring to room temperature, stir to recombine, and garnish before serving

WHITE BEAN AND ROASTED GARLIC DIP
WITH ROSEMARY

1 large garlic head, papery outer skins removed, head kept intact

Extra-virgin olive oil for drizzling, plus 3 Tbsp

Fine sea salt and freshly ground black pepper

Two 15-oz [425-g] cans cannellini beans, rinsed and drained

1½ tsp minced fresh rosemary

¼ cup [20 g] grated Parmigiano-Reggiano cheese

1½ Tbsp freshly squeezed lemon juice, plus more as needed

1 Tbsp water

Preheat the oven to 350°F [180°F].

Cut off the top quarter or so of the garlic head to expose the cloves. Cut a small sheet of aluminum foil and set the garlic on top, cut-side up. Lightly drizzle the garlic with olive oil and sprinkle with salt and pepper. Seal the edges of the foil and bake until the garlic cloves are soft and creamy, about 50 minutes. Set aside until cool enough to handle. Pull apart the garlic cloves and remove the skins, saving only the creamy flesh.

In a food processor, combine the garlic, beans, rosemary, Parmigiano, lemon juice, water, ½ tsp salt, and ¼ tsp pepper. Process to a thick purée, about 1 minute, scraping down the bowl once or twice. With the machine running, stream in the 3 Tbsp olive oil and continue to process until the mixture is smooth, creamy, and homogenous, about 30 seconds. Taste and adjust the seasoning with more salt, pepper, and lemon juice, if needed.

Transfer the dip to a wide, shallow bowl for serving. Cover and let stand at room temperature for about 30 minutes to allow the flavors to meld.

Use the back of a spoon to swirl the surface of the dip. Drizzle with olive oil and serve.

MAKES / about 2⅓ cups [590 g]

SERVE WITH / Crackers, crudités, fresh or toasted baguette slices, grissini, pita bread, pita chips

STORAGE / Best served the day it's made, but can be refrigerated without garnish for up to 2 days (color will dull with storage); bring to room temperature, stir to recombine, and garnish before serving

FAVA BEAN AND ROASTED FENNEL DIP
WITH GOAT CHEESE AND CHIVES

1 large fennel bulb

2 Tbsp extra-virgin olive oil

Fine sea salt and freshly ground black pepper

2 cups [280 g] frozen shelled fava beans

4 oz [115 g] goat cheese, crumbled

2 Tbsp freshly squeezed lemon juice

3 Tbsp minced fresh chives, plus more for garnish

Preheat the oven to 400°F [200°C].

Trim the bottom of the fennel bulb and cut off the stalks; if you like, reserve some fronds for garnish. If the outer layer of the bulb is bruised, remove and discard it. Cut the bulb from top to bottom into slices ⅜ in [1 cm] thick. It's fine if some of the layers separate.

In a medium bowl, toss the fennel with 1 Tbsp of the olive oil and a sprinkle of salt and pepper. Lay the slices in a single layer on a rimmed baking sheet and roast until the fennel is completely tender and some of the edges are browned, about 20 minutes. Let cool to room temperature on the baking sheet.

In a medium saucepan, bring 4 cups [960 ml] water to a boil over high heat. Add the fava beans and 2 tsp salt and return to a boil. Try a bean to make sure it's completely tender; if it isn't, continue to cook for 1 or 2 minutes (if undercooked, the beans won't purée nicely). Once the beans are tender, drain in a colander and run cold water over them until cool to the touch. Drain well and then transfer the beans to a food processor.

Add the cooled roasted fennel to the food processor. Pulse a few times, just until the beans and fennel are coarsely chopped. Scrape down the bowl and add the goat cheese, lemon juice, remaining 1 Tbsp olive oil, ¾ tsp salt, and ½ tsp pepper. Process until the mixture is as smooth as it can be, 1½ to 2 minutes, scraping down the bowl two or three times. Taste and adjust the seasoning with more salt and pepper, if needed.

Transfer the dip to a wide, shallow bowl for serving and stir in the chives. Cover and let stand at room temperature for about 30 minutes to allow the flavors to meld.

Use the back of a spoon to swirl the surface of the dip. Garnish with additional chives and fennel fronds (if using) and serve.

MAKES / about 2⅔ cups [700 g]

SERVE WITH / Crackers, crudités, fresh or toasted baguette slices, grissini, pita bread

STORAGE / Can be refrigerated without garnish for up to 2 days; bring to room temperature, stir to recombine, and garnish before serving

LIMA BEAN DIP
WITH PECORINO, BLACK PEPPER, AND LEMON

One 1-lb [455-g] bag frozen baby lima beans

Fine sea salt

½ cup plus 2 Tbsp [50 g] grated Pecorino Romano cheese

1 small garlic clove, germ removed (see page 9), chopped

1½ tsp finely grated lemon zest, plus 3 Tbsp freshly squeezed lemon juice

Freshly ground black pepper

¼ cup [60 ml] extra-virgin olive oil, plus more for drizzling

In a medium saucepan, bring 4 cups [960 ml] water to a boil over high heat. Add the lima beans and 2 tsp salt, return to a boil, and cook until the beans are completely tender, about 10 minutes (if undercooked, the beans won't purée nicely). Reserve about 2 Tbsp of the cooking water. Drain the beans in a colander and run cold water over them until cool to the touch. Drain well and then transfer the beans to a food processor.

Add the Pecorino, garlic, lemon zest, lemon juice, ¾ tsp salt, 1 tsp pepper, and the reserved cooking water to the food processor. Process to a thick purée, 15 to 20 seconds, scraping down the bowl as needed. With the machine running, stream in the olive oil and continue to process until the mixture is as smooth as it can be, about 45 seconds, scraping down the bowl once or twice. Taste and adjust the seasoning with more salt and pepper, if needed.

Transfer the dip to a wide, shallow bowl for serving. Cover and let stand at room temperature for about 30 minutes to allow the flavors to meld.

Use the back of a spoon to swirl the surface of the dip. Drizzle with olive oil, grind additional pepper over the top, and serve.

Rustic, subtly sweet, a touch nutty, spicy (depending on the heat of the chiles), slightly bitter

MAKES / about 2 cups [460 g]

SERVE WITH / Crackers, pita chips, toasted baguette slices

STORAGE / Can be refrigerated without garnish for up to 2 days; bring to room temperature, stir to recombine, and garnish before serving

EDAMAME DIP
WITH CHARRED GREEN ONIONS AND JALAPEÑOS

8 oz [230 g] frozen shelled edamame

Fine sea salt

2 large bunches green onions, trimmed

Mild-flavored extra-virgin olive oil for brushing, plus 3 Tbsp and more for drizzling

2 jalapeño chiles, stemmed, halved lengthwise, seeded, and ribs removed

1 medium garlic clove, germ removed (see page 9), chopped

2½ Tbsp freshly squeezed lemon juice

½ tsp ground cumin

¼ tsp cayenne pepper

Freshly ground black pepper

In a medium saucepan, bring 4 cups [960 ml] water to a boil over high heat. Add the edamame and 2 tsp salt, return to a boil, and cook until the edamame are completely tender, about 5 minutes (if undercooked, the beans won't purée nicely). Reserve 3 Tbsp of the cooking water. Drain the edamame in a colander and run cold water over them until cool to the touch. Drain well and then set aside.

Position an oven rack so that it is about 3 in [7.5 cm] from the broiler and preheat the broiler.

Brush the green onions lightly with olive oil and arrange them in a single layer on a large rimmed baking sheet. Turn each jalapeño half skin-side up, press down on it with the palm of your hand to flatten, and lightly brush with oil. Arrange the jalapeño halves skin-side up on the baking sheet next to the green onions.

Broil the green onions and chiles until the green onions are lightly charred, 3 to 5 minutes (watch carefully—cooking times will vary based on the heat of the broiler and the moisture content of the onions). Using tongs, flip the green onions and continue to broil until the second sides are charred and the skins on the chiles are blistered and blackened, 3 to 5 minutes longer; some dry, completely

CONTINUED

burnt pieces of green onion are fine. Remove any onions that are done ahead of the others. If the chiles are not yet charred when the onions are done, continue to broil them.

Let the onions and chiles rest until cool enough to handle. Cut the onions into rough 1-in [2.5-cm] lengths. Remove the skins from the chiles.

Measure out and reserve a generous 1 Tbsp edamame for garnish.

In a food processor, combine the remaining edamame, the green onions, chiles, garlic, lemon juice, cumin, cayenne, ¾ tsp salt, ¼ tsp black pepper, and the reserved cooking water. Process to a thick purée, about 1 minute, scraping down the bowl as needed. With the machine running, stream in the 3 Tbsp olive oil and continue to process until the mixture is as smooth as it can be, 1½ to 2 minutes, scraping down the bowl as needed. Taste and adjust the seasoning with more salt and pepper, if needed.

Transfer the dip to a wide, shallow bowl for serving. Cover and let stand at room temperature for about 30 minutes to allow the flavors to meld.

Use the back of a spoon to swirl the surface of the dip. Scatter the reserved edamame on top, drizzle with olive oil, and serve.

MAKES / about 2¾ cups [715 g]

SERVE WITH / Crackers, grissini, pita bread, pita chips, toasted baguette slices

STORAGE / Can be refrigerated without garnish for up to 3 days; bring to room temperature, stir to recombine, and garnish before serving

LENTIL DIP
WITH CARAMELIZED ONIONS AND YOGURT

1 cup [190 g] brown lentils

1 cup [240 ml] low-sodium chicken broth or vegetable broth

1 dried bay leaf

One 1-in [2.5-cm] cinnamon stick

Fine sea salt

1¼ lb [570 g] sweet onions

⅓ cup [80 ml] extra-virgin olive oil, plus more for drizzling

2 large garlic cloves, minced

1¼ tsp ground cumin

¾ tsp ground coriander

⅛ tsp ground cinnamon

Freshly ground black pepper

2 Tbsp freshly squeezed lemon juice

¼ cup [60 g] plain whole-milk yogurt (see Note)

¼ cup [15 g] chopped fresh flat-leaf parsley, plus torn leaves for garnish

In a medium saucepan, combine 3 cups [720 ml] water, the lentils, chicken broth, bay leaf, cinnamon stick, and ¼ tsp salt. Bring to a boil over high heat, and then turn the heat to medium and simmer, stirring occasionally, until the lentils are tender, about 30 minutes. Let the lentils cool in the pan for about 10 minutes; this will ensure they are soft and fully tender so they will purée nicely.

Drain the lentils in a large fine-mesh strainer, discarding the cooking liquid. Let the lentils cool to room temperature. Remove and discard the bay leaf and cinnamon stick.

While the lentils simmer, halve the onions lengthwise (with the grain) and peel. Set each onion half on its cut side and halve again lengthwise. Cut each onion quarter crosswise (against the grain) into very thin slices.

In a large skillet over medium-high heat, warm the olive oil until shimmering. Add the onions and ¼ tsp salt and stir until the onions are coated with oil. Cook, stirring occasionally, until the onions are completely softened and begin to brown and stick to the bottom of the pan, about 25 minutes. Continue to cook, now stirring more frequently and scraping the bottom of the pan, until the onions are richly caramelized, 15 to 20 minutes more; lower the heat if the onions begin to color very unevenly. Add the garlic, cumin, coriander, and ground cinnamon and turn off the heat. Stir to incorporate the garlic and spices, allowing them to cook with the pan's residual heat. Set the pan aside.

Transfer the lentils to a food processor and add ½ tsp salt and ½ tsp pepper. Process until the lentils are as smooth as they can be, 1 to 1½ minutes, scraping down the bowl once or twice. Transfer to a medium bowl and add the caramelized onions along with any oil in the pan, the lemon juice, yogurt, and parsley and stir until well combined. Taste and adjust the seasoning with more salt and pepper, if needed.

Transfer the dip to a wide, shallow bowl for serving. Cover and let stand at room temperature for about 30 minutes to allow the flavors to meld.

Use the back of a spoon to swirl the surface of the dip. Drizzle with olive oil, garnish with parsley, and serve.

NOTE / *This recipe uses regular yogurt instead of Greek yogurt because it helps thin the puréed lentils' thick consistency. You can use Greek yogurt if that's what you have on hand, but you'll need to stir 1 to 2 Tbsp water into the dip along with the yogurt.*

VEGETABLES
&
HERBS

MAKES / about 1⅔ cups [360 g]

SERVE WITH / Crackers, crudités, grissini, pita chips, roasted potatoes, toasted baguette slices

STORAGE / Best served the day it's made, but can be refrigerated without garnish for up to 2 days (color will dull with storage); bring to room temperature, stir to recombine, and garnish before serving

ARTICHOKE-BASIL PESTO
WITH WALNUTS AND LEMON

½ cup [55 g] chopped walnuts

One 14-oz [400-g] can artichoke hearts, drained and patted dry

1¼ cups [25 g] packed fresh basil leaves

¼ cup [20 g] grated Parmigiano-Reggiano cheese

¾ tsp finely grated lemon zest, plus 1 Tbsp freshly squeezed lemon juice

1 medium garlic clove, germ removed (see page 9), chopped

Fine sea salt and freshly ground black pepper

⅓ cup [80 ml] extra-virgin olive oil, plus more for drizzling

In a small skillet over medium heat, toast the walnuts, stirring frequently, until fragrant and golden, 6 to 8 minutes. Transfer to a food processor and let cool.

Add the artichokes, basil, Parmigiano, lemon zest, lemon juice, garlic, ½ tsp salt, and ¼ tsp pepper to the food processor. Process to a thick purée, about 45 seconds, scraping down the bowl as needed. With the machine running, stream in the olive oil and continue to process until the mixture is as smooth as it can be, about 30 seconds, scraping down the bowl as needed. Taste and adjust the seasoning with more salt and pepper, if needed.

Transfer the pesto to a wide, shallow bowl for serving. Cover and let stand at room temperature for about 30 minutes to allow the flavors to meld.

Use the back of a spoon to swirl the surface of the dip. Drizzle with olive oil and serve.

MAKES / about 2 cups [400 g]

SERVE WITH / Crackers, pita chips, toasted baguette slices

STORAGE / Can be refrigerated without garnish for up to 3 days; bring to room temperature, stir to recombine, and garnish before serving

MUSHROOM PESTO
WITH PARSLEY AND THYME

Scant ¼ cup [5 g] dried porcini mushrooms

½ cup [120 ml] boiling water

3 Tbsp pine nuts

1 lb [455 g] cremini mushrooms, sliced about ¼ in [6 mm] thick

5 Tbsp extra-virgin olive oil, plus more for drizzling

Fine sea salt

2 medium garlic cloves, chopped

¼ cup [20 g] grated Parmigiano-Reggiano cheese

¼ cup [5 g] packed fresh flat-leaf parsley leaves

2 tsp fresh thyme leaves, plus more for garnish

1 Tbsp freshly squeezed lemon juice

Freshly ground black pepper

Preheat the oven to 500°F [260°C].

While the oven heats, put the porcini mushrooms in a small heatproof bowl and cover with the boiling water. Set aside to hydrate.

In a small skillet over medium heat, toast the pine nuts, stirring frequently, until fragrant and golden, about 5 minutes. Transfer 2 Tbsp of the pine nuts to a food processor and reserve the remaining 1 Tbsp for garnish.

In a medium bowl, toss the cremini mushrooms with 2 Tbsp of the olive oil and ¼ tsp salt. Distribute in an even layer on a rimmed baking sheet. Roast the mushrooms until they have released their moisture and are shrunken in size, about 5 minutes. Stir and continue to roast until most of the moisture on the baking sheet has evaporated but the mushrooms themselves are still quite moist, 5 to 6 minutes; do not let them dry out. Turn off the oven and stir the garlic into the hot mushrooms. Return the baking sheet to the oven for 1 minute to allow the garlic to cook. Remove from the oven and let the mushroom mixture cool on the baking sheet.

Using a fork or slotted spoon, lift the porcini mushrooms from their soaking liquid and add them to the food processor; reserve the soaking liquid.

When the roasted mushrooms have cooled, add them to the food processor along with the Parmigiano, parsley, thyme, lemon juice, ½ tsp salt, ½ tsp black pepper, and 1 Tbsp of the porcini liquid (be careful to avoid the sediment that collects at the bottom of the bowl). Pulse about eight times, until the mixture is coarsely chopped. Scrape down the bowl. With the machine running, stream in the remaining 3 Tbsp olive oil and continue to process until the mixture is as smooth as it can be, about 1 minute, scraping down the bowl once or twice. Taste and adjust the seasoning with more salt and pepper, if needed.

Transfer the pesto to a wide, shallow bowl for serving. Cover and let stand at room temperature for about 30 minutes to allow the flavors to meld.

Use the back of a spoon to swirl the surface of the dip. Sprinkle with the reserved pine nuts and thyme leaves, drizzle lightly with olive oil, and serve.

Thick, creamy, tangy, mineral-ly, slightly herbaceous

MAKES / about 3¼ cups [785 g]

SERVE WITH / Crackers, pita chips, toasted baguette slices

STORAGE / Best served the day it's made, but can be refrigerated without garnish for up to 2 days (spinach will dull slightly in color); bring to room temperature, stir to recombine, and garnish before serving

SPINACH DIP
WITH YOGURT AND FETA

2 cups [480 g] whole-milk Greek yogurt

4 oz [115 g] feta cheese, finely crumbled

½ tsp finely grated lemon zest, plus 1½ Tbsp freshly squeezed lemon juice

Fine sea salt and freshly ground black pepper

2 Tbsp extra-virgin olive oil, plus more for drizzling

3 green onions (white and green parts), thinly sliced

1 Tbsp finely chopped fresh dill, plus more for garnish

2 medium garlic cloves, germ removed (see page 9), minced to a paste

Big pinch of ground nutmeg

One 10-oz [280-g] box frozen chopped spinach, completely thawed and wrung in a clean kitchen towel until very dry

In a medium bowl, combine the yogurt, feta, lemon zest, ¾ tsp salt, and ½ tsp pepper, mashing the feta with a rubber spatula until the mixture is relatively smooth. Stir in the olive oil, lemon juice, green onions, dill, garlic, and nutmeg. Break apart the clump of squeezed spinach and add to the yogurt mixture. Stir with the spatula until the spinach is well incorporated. Taste and adjust the seasoning with more salt and pepper, if needed.

Transfer the dip to a wide, shallow bowl for serving. Cover and let stand at room temperature for about 30 minutes to allow the flavors to meld.

Use the back of a spoon to swirl the surface of the dip. Drizzle with olive oil, sprinkle with a little more black pepper and dill, and serve.

MAKES / about 2 cups [500 g]

SERVE WITH / Crackers, crudités, fresh or toasted baguette slices, pita bread, pita chips

STORAGE / Can be refrigerated without garnish for up to 5 days (flavor improves with storage); bring to room temperature, stir to recombine, and garnish before serving

EGGPLANT AND YOGURT DIP
WITH SAFFRON

¼ tsp saffron threads, crumbled

2 tsp warm water

2 lb [910 g] globe eggplants

2 Tbsp pine nuts

2 Tbsp extra-virgin olive oil, plus more for drizzling

1 sweet onion, finely chopped

Fine sea salt

2 medium garlic cloves, minced

¾ cup [180 g] whole-milk Greek yogurt

2 tsp freshly squeezed lemon juice

Freshly ground black pepper

1 Tbsp chopped fresh flat-leaf parsley

Position an oven rack so that it is about 8 in [20 cm] from the broiler and preheat the broiler. Line a rimmed baking sheet with aluminum foil.

Combine the saffron and water in a small bowl and set aside to allow the saffron flavor to bloom.

Pierce each eggplant a few times with the tip of a paring knife to prevent it from bursting in the oven and set on the prepared baking sheet. Broil the eggplants, using tongs to rotate them every 10 minutes, until charred all over and completely collapsed, 45 to 50 minutes. Let cool on the baking sheet for 20 to 30 minutes.

In a small skillet over medium heat, toast the pine nuts, stirring frequently, until fragrant and golden, about 5 minutes. Set aside to cool.

Set a colander in a large bowl. Trim off and discard the tops of the eggplants. Slit them lengthwise and use a spoon to scoop the pulp into the colander; make sure to scrape off any pulp that clings to the skin. Let the pulp drain for 15 minutes, shaking the colander occasionally to release the moisture.

Transfer the eggplant to a cutting board and finely chop with a chef's knife. Set aside.

In a medium skillet over medium-high heat, warm the olive oil. Add the onion and a pinch of salt and cook, stirring frequently, until the onion is caramelized, 8 to 10 minutes. Turn the heat to medium-low, add the garlic, and cook, stirring constantly, until the garlic no longer smells raw, about 1 minute. Add the eggplant and the saffron water and cook, stirring to combine, until any excess moisture has evaporated, about 3 minutes. Transfer to a medium bowl and let cool until barely warm to the touch.

Add the yogurt, lemon juice, ¾ tsp salt, and ¼ tsp pepper to the mixture and stir well. Taste and adjust the seasoning with more salt and pepper, if needed.

Transfer the dip to a wide, shallow bowl for serving. Cover and let stand at room temperature for about 30 minutes to allow the flavors to meld.

Use the back of a spoon to swirl the surface of the dip. Sprinkle the pine nuts and parsley over the top, drizzle with olive oil, and serve.

Smoky, lightly lemony, subtly sweet, fruity

MAKES / about 2⅓ cups [590 g]

SERVE WITH / Crackers, crudités, fresh or toasted baguette slices, pita bread, pita chips

STORAGE / Can be refrigerated without garnish for up to 5 days; bring to room temperature, stir to recombine, and garnish before serving

EGGPLANT DIP WITH TAHINI
(BABA GHANOUSH)

3 lb [1.4 kg] globe eggplants

2½ Tbsp freshly squeezed lemon juice, plus more as needed

2 Tbsp tahini

1 medium garlic clove, germ removed (see page 9), chopped

¼ tsp smoked paprika, plus more for sprinkling (see Note)

Fine sea salt

3 Tbsp extra-virgin olive oil, plus more for drizzling

Build a medium-hot fire in a charcoal grill or preheat a gas grill to medium-high. Alternatively, adjust an oven rack so that it is positioned about 8 in [20 cm] from the broiler and preheat the broiler. If using a broiler, line a rimmed baking sheet with aluminum foil.

Pierce each eggplant a few times with the tip of a paring knife to prevent it from bursting during cooking. Grill the eggplants directly over the fire, using tongs to rotate them every 5 minutes, until charred all over and completely collapsed, about 30 minutes. If using a broiler, set the eggplants on the prepared baking sheet and broil, using tongs to rotate them every 10 minutes, until charred all over and completely collapsed, 45 to 50 minutes. Let the eggplants cool for 20 to 30 minutes.

Set a colander in a large bowl. Trim off and discard the tops of the eggplants. Slit them lengthwise and use a spoon to scoop the pulp into the colander; make sure to scrape off any pulp that clings to the skin. Let the pulp drain for 15 minutes, shaking the colander occasionally to release the moisture.

Transfer the eggplant to a food processor and add the lemon juice, tahini, garlic, smoked paprika, and 1 tsp salt. Process to a smooth purée, 45 to 60 seconds, scraping down the bowl once or twice. With the machine running, stream in the olive oil and continue to process until the mixture is as smooth as it can be, about 1 minute, scraping down the bowl once or twice. Taste and adjust the seasoning with more salt and lemon juice, if needed.

Transfer the dip to a wide, shallow bowl for serving. Cover and let stand at room temperature for about 1 hour to allow the flavors to meld.

Use the back of a spoon to swirl the surface of the dip. Drizzle with olive oil, sprinkle with smoked paprika, and serve.

NOTE / *Smoked paprika is not a traditional ingredient in baba ghanoush, but it enhances the smoky flavor of the charred eggplant.*

Aromatic, warmly spiced, savory with sweet notes, herbaceous

MAKES / about 3¼ cups [760 g]

SERVE WITH / Crackers, lavash, naan, pita bread, pita chips

STORAGE / Can be refrigerated without garnish for up to 5 days; bring to room temperature, stir to recombine, and garnish before serving

SPICED EGGPLANT AND TOMATO DIP

2 lb [910 g] globe eggplants

1 lb [455 g] plum tomatoes

1½ Tbsp extra-virgin olive oil

1 small onion, minced

1 jalapeño chile, stemmed, seeded, and minced

2 medium garlic cloves, minced

1 tsp grated fresh ginger

1 tsp garam masala

½ tsp ground turmeric

Fine sea salt and freshly ground black pepper

2 tsp freshly squeezed lemon juice

3 Tbsp chopped fresh cilantro, plus more for garnish

Position an oven rack so that it is about 8 in [20 cm] from the broiler and preheat the broiler. Line a rimmed baking sheet with aluminum foil.

Pierce each eggplant a few times with the tip of a paring knife to prevent it from bursting in the oven and set on one side of the prepared baking sheet. Set the tomatoes on the other side. Broil, using tongs to rotate the eggplants after 10 minutes (no need to rotate the tomatoes). Continue to broil for 10 minutes more, then transfer the tomatoes to a plate to cool. Rotate the eggplants again and continue to broil, rotating every 10 minutes, until charred all over and completely collapsed, 25 to 30 minutes more. (If the tomatoes left behind juices that are beginning to scorch and smoke, fold over the foil to cover or set the eggplants on top of those areas.) Let cool on the baking sheet for 20 to 30 minutes.

While the eggplants cool, peel and chop the tomatoes, reserving their juice along with the pulp.

CONTINUED

Set a colander in a large bowl. Trim off and discard the tops of the eggplants. Slit them lengthwise and use a spoon to scoop the pulp into the colander; make sure to scrape off any pulp that clings to the skin. Let the pulp drain for 15 minutes, shaking the colander occasionally to release the moisture.

Transfer the eggplant to a cutting board and finely chop with a chef's knife. Set aside.

In a large skillet over medium heat, warm the olive oil until shimmering. Add the onion and jalapeño and cook, stirring occasionally, until softened but not browned, 6 to 8 minutes. Add the garlic, ginger, garam masala, and turmeric and cook, stirring constantly, until the garlic no longer smells raw, about 1 minute. Add the tomatoes with their juice, increase the heat to medium-high, and cook until most of the moisture evaporates, 2 to 3 minutes. Add the eggplant, 1 tsp salt, and ½ tsp pepper and stir well to combine. Cook the mixture, stirring occasionally, until quite dry and thick and the flavors have melded, 6 to 8 minutes. Transfer to a bowl and let cool completely.

Add the lemon juice and cilantro to the mixture and stir well. Taste and adjust the seasoning with more salt and pepper, if needed.

Transfer the dip to a wide, shallow bowl for serving. Garnish with cilantro and serve.

MAKES / about 1½ cups [370 g]

SERVE WITH / Crackers (great with seeded or multigrain), crudités, fresh or toasted baguette slices, pita bread, pita chips

STORAGE / Can be refrigerated without garnish for up to 3 days; bring to room temperature, stir to recombine, and garnish before serving

ROASTED RED PEPPER AND WALNUT DIP WITH POMEGRANATE MOLASSES (MUHAMMARA)

¾ cup [85 g] walnuts

4½ Tbsp [70 ml] extra-virgin olive oil, plus more for drizzling

¼ cup [35 g] unseasoned dried bread crumbs

2 medium garlic cloves, minced

¾ tsp ground cumin

½ tsp paprika

¼ tsp cayenne pepper

1 cup [200 g] drained jarred roasted red peppers, patted dry

1 Tbsp pomegranate molasses

½ tsp fresh lemon juice

Fine sea salt and freshly ground black pepper

In a medium skillet over medium heat, toast the walnuts, stirring frequently, until fragrant and lightly browned, about 5 minutes. Set aside 2 Tbsp for garnish. Transfer the remaining walnuts to a food processor.

In the same skillet, stir together 1½ Tbsp of the olive oil and the bread crumbs. Fry the crumbs over medium-high heat, stirring frequently, until golden, about 5 minutes. Turn off the heat; add the garlic, cumin, paprika, and cayenne; and mash the garlic and spices into the crumbs, allowing them to cook in the pan's residual heat, until the garlic no longer smells raw, about 1 minute. Transfer the mixture to the food processor with the walnuts and let cool. Pulse ten to twelve times, until the mixture is finely ground.

Add the red peppers, pomegranate molasses, lemon juice, ¾ tsp salt, and ¼ tsp black pepper to the food processor. Process to a thick purée, 30 to 45 seconds, scraping down the bowl as needed. With the machine running, stream in the remaining 3 Tbsp olive oil and continue to process until the mixture is as smooth as it can be, about 1 minute,

CONTINUED

scraping down the bowl once or twice. Taste and adjust the seasoning with more salt and pepper, if needed.

Transfer the dip to a wide, shallow bowl for serving. Cover and let stand at room temperature for about 1 hour to allow the flavors to meld.

Use the back of a spoon to swirl the surface of the dip. Coarsely chop the reserved nuts and sprinkle over the top. Drizzle with olive oil and serve.

Rich, thick, smoky, bittersweet, concentrated, intense

MAKES / about 2 cups [500 g]

SERVE WITH / Crudités, pita chips, toasted baguette slices

STORAGE / Can be refrigerated without garnish for up to 3 days; bring to room temperature, stir to recombine, and garnish before serving

ROASTED RED PEPPER AND ANCHO DIP
WITH ALMONDS AND SMOKED PAPRIKA

2 ancho chiles

⅔ cup [80 g] blanched slivered almonds

4 Tbsp extra-virgin olive oil

¼ cup [35 g] unseasoned dried bread crumbs

3 medium garlic cloves, minced

1 tsp smoked paprika

¾ cup [150 g] drained jarred roasted red peppers, patted dry

½ cup [120 g] well-drained canned diced fire-roasted tomatoes

1 Tbsp sherry vinegar

Fine sea salt and freshly ground black pepper

Put the chiles in a heatproof bowl. Cover with boiling water, place a small plate on top to keep the chiles submerged, and let soak for about 20 minutes to soften.

Meanwhile, in a medium skillet over medium-high heat, toast the almonds, stirring frequently, until fragrant and deep golden, about 5 minutes. Set aside 2 Tbsp for garnish. Transfer the remaining almonds to a food processor.

In the same skillet, stir together 1½ Tbsp of the olive oil and the bread crumbs. Fry the crumbs over medium-high heat, stirring frequently, until golden, about 5 minutes. Turn off the heat, add the garlic and smoked paprika, and mash the garlic and paprika into the crumbs, allowing them to cook in the pan's residual heat, until the garlic no longer smells raw, about 1 minute. Transfer the mixture to the food processor with the almonds and let cool. Pulse ten to twelve times, until the mixture is finely ground.

Remove the chiles from the soaking water. Pull off the stems, wipe out the seeds, and tear the flesh into pieces. Add the chile pieces, the red peppers, tomatoes, vinegar, 1 tsp salt, and ¼ tsp pepper to the food processor. Process to a thick purée, 45 to 60 seconds, scraping down the bowl as needed. With the machine running, stream in the remaining 2½ Tbsp olive oil and continue to process until the mixture is as smooth as it can be, about 1 minute, scraping down the bowl once or twice. Taste and adjust the seasoning with more salt and pepper, if needed.

Transfer the dip to a wide, shallow bowl for serving. Cover and let stand at room temperature for about 1 hour to allow the flavors to meld.

Use the back of a spoon to swirl the surface of the dip. Coarsely chop the reserved almonds, sprinkle over the dip, and serve.

MAKES / about 4 cups [730 g]

SERVE WITH / Chips, crackers, fresh or toasted baguette slices

STORAGE / Best served right away, but can be assembled and refrigerated in the baking dish for up to 3 hours; bring to room temperature and sprinkle with Parmigiano just before broiling

WARM CHARRED BRUSSELS SPROUTS DIP
WITH RICOTTA AND BACON

3 slices thick-cut bacon, finely chopped

1 medium garlic clove, minced

1 lb [455 g] Brussels sprouts

4 Tbsp extra-virgin olive oil

Fine sea salt and freshly ground black pepper

1½ cups [360 g] whole-milk ricotta cheese, at room temperature

½ cup [40 g] grated Parmigiano-Reggiano cheese, plus 2 Tbsp

3 green onions (white and green parts), thinly sliced

1 tsp finely grated lemon zest, plus 2½ Tbsp freshly squeezed lemon juice

Position an oven rack in the lower third of the oven. Place a rimmed baking sheet on the rack and preheat the oven to 500°F [260°C]. Lightly oil a shallow, broiler-safe 4-cup [960-ml] baking dish or gratin dish.

In a medium skillet over medium heat, fry the bacon until browned and the fat has been rendered, about 8 minutes. Add the garlic and cook, stirring constantly, until the garlic no longer smells raw, about 1 minute. Using a slotted spoon, transfer to a paper towel–lined plate to drain.

Trim the bases of the Brussels sprouts and discard any blemished and discolored outer leaves. If any good leaves fall off, reserve them. Cut each sprout in half lengthwise.

Fit a food processor with the medium (4-mm) slicing disk and slice the sprouts and any loose leaves by feeding them through the feed tube. Alternatively, use a sharp chef's knife to very thinly slice the sprouts and leaves by hand. Put the sliced sprouts in a medium bowl. Drizzle with 2 Tbsp of the olive oil and sprinkle with ¼ tsp salt and a few grinds of pepper. Toss until well coated with oil.

CONTINUED

Carefully remove the hot baking sheet from the oven and empty the sprouts onto it, distributing them in an even layer. Roast the sprouts until they are a mixture of crisp, darkly charred bits and tender green shreds, 13 to 15 minutes, stirring every 4 to 5 minutes. Let cool on the baking sheet.

Preheat the broiler.

In a medium bowl, combine the ricotta, ½ cup [40 g] Parmigiano, green onions, lemon zest, lemon juice, bacon-garlic mixture, remaining 2 Tbsp olive oil, 1 tsp salt, and ½ tsp pepper. Stir until well combined. Add the charred sprouts and mix until fully incorporated. Taste and adjust the seasoning with more salt and pepper, if needed.

Transfer the dip to the prepared baking dish and spread into an even layer, leaving peaks and valleys on the surface for nice browning. Sprinkle with the remaining 2 Tbsp Parmigiano.

Broil the dip until browned on top, sizzling around the edges, and just warmed through, 4 to 5 minutes. Serve hot.

Rustic, fragrant, savory-sweet, slightly spicy

MAKES / about 3⅓ cups [810 g]

SERVE WITH / Crackers, lavash, naan, pita bread, pita chips

STORAGE / Can be refrigerated without garnish for up to 3 days; bring to room temperature, stir to recombine, and garnish before serving

CURRIED CAULIFLOWER DIP

⅓ cup [50 g] golden raisins

4 Tbsp [60 ml] extra-virgin olive oil

2 tsp curry powder

Fine sea salt and freshly ground black pepper

One 2-lb [910-g] head cauliflower

1 jalapeño chile, stemmed, quartered lengthwise, seeded, and ribs removed

3 medium garlic cloves, unpeeled, woody ends trimmed

½ cup [70 g] raw cashews

½ cup [60 g] plain whole-milk yogurt

2½ Tbsp freshly squeezed lemon juice, plus more as needed

½ tsp grated fresh ginger

¼ cup [15 g] minced fresh cilantro, plus torn leaves for garnish

Preheat the oven to 400°F [200°C].

Put the raisins in a small bowl and add warm water to cover. Set aside to allow raisins to plump up.

In a large bowl, mix together 2 Tbsp of the olive oil, the curry powder, ½ tsp salt, and ¼ tsp pepper.

Using a chef's knife, cut the cauliflower lengthwise into quarters and cut away the tough core and stem (with leafy parts) from each quarter. Set each quarter on its side and cut lengthwise into pieces ½ in [12 mm] thick. It's fine if some of the pieces fall apart.

Put the cauliflower pieces and jalapeño quarters into the bowl with the curry oil and toss until evenly coated. Distribute in an even layer on a rimmed baking sheet, and add the garlic cloves. Roast for 15 minutes, then remove the baking sheet from the oven, scatter the cashews over the vegetables, and stir to combine. Continue to roast until a skewer inserted into the thickest part of a piece of cauliflower meets no resistance, about 15 minutes more. Let cool completely on the baking sheet.

CONTINUED

Remove the garlic cloves and peel them. Put the garlic and the cauliflower mixture in a food processor and add the yogurt, lemon juice, ginger, ½ tsp salt, and ¼ tsp pepper. Process to a thick purée, about 1 minute, scraping down the bowl once or twice. With the machine running, stream in the remaining 2 Tbsp olive oil and continue to process until the mixture is as smooth as it can be, about 1 minute, scraping down the bowl as needed.

Transfer the dip to a medium bowl. Drain the raisins, pat them dry, and chop coarsely. Stir the raisins and cilantro into the dip. Taste and adjust the seasoning with more salt, pepper, and lemon juice, if needed.

Transfer the dip to a wide, shallow bowl for serving. Cover and let stand at room temperature for about 30 minutes to allow the flavors to meld.

Use the back of a spoon to swirl the surface of the dip. Garnish with cilantro leaves and serve.

MAKES / about 2¼ cups [540 g]

SERVE WITH / Crackers, pita bread, pita chips, toasted baguette slices

STORAGE / Can be refrigerated without garnish for up to 5 days; bring to room temperature, stir to recombine, and garnish before serving

CARROT DIP
WITH NORTH AFRICAN SPICES

1½ lb [680 g] carrots, peeled and cut into rounds ½ in [12 mm] thick

1 tsp paprika

½ tsp ground coriander

½ tsp ground cumin

¼ tsp ground ginger

¼ tsp cayenne pepper

¼ tsp freshly ground black pepper

⅛ tsp ground cinnamon

2 Tbsp freshly squeezed lemon juice

1 medium garlic clove, germ removed (see page 9), chopped

Fine sea salt

3 Tbsp extra-virgin olive oil, plus more for drizzling

3 Tbsp chopped or slivered pitted green olives

1 Tbsp chopped fresh cilantro or flat-leaf parsley (optional)

Fit a large saucepan with a steamer basket and add enough water to fill the bottom of the pan without touching the basket. Bring to a boil over medium-high heat. Add the carrots in an even layer. Cover and steam until the tip of a knife meets no resistance when inserted into a carrot, 15 to 18 minutes, stirring once about halfway through. Remove the basket from the pan and let the carrots cool to room temperature.

In a small skillet over medium heat, combine the paprika, coriander, cumin, ginger, cayenne, black pepper, and cinnamon and toast, stirring constantly, until the spices are deeply fragrant, about 1 minute.

In a food processor, combine the carrots, toasted spices, lemon juice, garlic, and ¾ tsp salt. Process to a thick purée, about 20 seconds, scraping down the bowl once. With the machine running, stream in the olive oil and continue to process until the mixture is smooth and well combined, 15 to 20 seconds, scraping down the bowl once more. Taste and adjust the seasoning with more salt, if needed.

Transfer the dip to a wide, shallow bowl for serving.

Use the back of a spoon to swirl the surface of the dip. Sprinkle with the olives and cilantro (if using), drizzle with olive oil, and serve.

Richly colored, rustic, earthy, tangy-sweet

MAKES / about 2⅓ cups [580 g]

SERVE WITH / Crackers, pita bread, pita chips

STORAGE / Can be refrigerated without garnish for up to 3 days; bring to room temperature, stir to recombine, and garnish before serving

BEET AND LABNEH DIP
WITH FETA AND PISTACHIOS

1 lb [455 g] red beets (without greens), scrubbed

½ cup [130 g] labneh (see page 86)

1 medium garlic clove, germ removed (see page 9), chopped

2 Tbsp extra-virgin olive oil

1½ tsp pomegranate molasses

¼ tsp ground coriander

Fine sea salt and freshly ground black pepper

1½ oz [40 g] feta cheese, crumbled

2 Tbsp salted roasted pistachios, coarsely chopped

1 to 2 Tbsp chopped fresh flat-leaf parsley (optional)

Preheat the oven to 350°F [180°C].

Put the beets in a small baking dish. Add ¼ cup [60 ml] water and cover tightly with foil. Roast until a metal skewer inserted into the largest beet meets absolutely no resistance, 1 to 1½ hours, depending on the size of the beets. Uncover and let cool to room temperature.

Slip the skins off the beets, using a paring knife to scrape off any areas that cling. Cut the beets into rough 1-in [2.5-cm] chunks and put them in a food processor. Add the labneh, garlic, olive oil, pomegranate molasses, coriander, ¾ tsp salt, and ½ tsp pepper. Process until the mixture is as smooth as it can be, about 1 minute, scraping down the bowl two or three times. Taste and adjust the seasoning with more salt and pepper, if needed.

Transfer the dip to a wide, shallow bowl for serving. Cover and let stand at room temperature for about 30 minutes to allow the flavors to meld.

Use the back of a spoon to swirl the surface of the dip. Sprinkle with the feta, pistachios, and parsley (if using) and serve.

NOTE / *The dip may separate slightly upon standing; stirring will bring it back together.*

MAKES / about 3 cups [760 g]

SERVE WITH / Crackers, crudités, pita bread, pita chips, toasted baguette slices

STORAGE / Can be refrigerated without garnish for up to 3 days; bring to room temperature, stir to recombine, and garnish before serving

CELERY ROOT DIP
WITH GARLIC AND ALMONDS

1¾ to 2 lb [800 to 910 g] celery root, trimmed, peeled, and cut into 1-in [2.5-cm] chunks

3 large garlic cloves, crushed and peeled, woody ends trimmed

⅓ cup [80 ml] extra-virgin olive oil, plus more for drizzling

¾ cup [80 g] sliced almonds

1½ Tbsp freshly squeezed lemon juice, plus more as needed

2 Tbsp water, plus more as needed

Fine sea salt and freshly ground black pepper

Fit a large saucepan with a steamer basket and add enough water to fill the bottom of the pan without touching the basket. Add the celery root in an even layer. Cover and bring to a boil over medium-high heat. Steam until the tip of a knife meets no resistance when inserted into one of the larger pieces of celery root, 10 to 12 minutes. Remove the basket from the pan and let the celery root cool to room temperature.

In a small saucepan over medium heat, combine the garlic and olive oil. Cook until the garlic is pale gold and quite tender, 6 to 7 minutes, adjusting the heat as needed to maintain a steady but gentle bubble. Remove the garlic from the oil and set aside both the garlic and oil to cool.

In a medium skillet over medium heat, toast the almonds, stirring frequently, until fragrant and lightly browned, 6 to 8 minutes. Set aside to cool.

Reserve 2 Tbsp of the almonds for garnish.

CONTINUED

In a food processor, combine the cooled celery root, the remaining almonds, garlic, lemon juice, water, 1 tsp salt, and ½ tsp pepper. Process to a thick, relatively smooth purée, 1 to 1½ minutes, scraping down the bowl once or twice. With the machine running, stream in the garlic-infused olive oil and continue to process until the mixture is as smooth as it can be, about 1 minute, scraping down the bowl as needed. Taste and adjust the seasoning with more salt, pepper, and lemon juice if needed; if the consistency is too thick, adjust by adding a little more water.

Transfer the dip to a wide, shallow bowl for serving. Cover and let stand at room temperature for about 30 minutes to allow the flavors to meld.

Use the back of a spoon to swirl the surface of the dip. Sprinkle with the reserved almonds, drizzle with olive oil, and serve.

MAKES / about 2½ cups [660 g]

SERVE WITH / Crackers (especially seeded crackers), pita chips, toasted baguette slices

STORAGE / Can be refrigerated without garnish for up to 3 days; bring to room temperature, stir to recombine, and garnish before serving

KABOCHA PUMPKIN DIP
WITH MAPLE, YOGURT, AND HARISSA

One 2-lb [910-g] kabocha pumpkin

2 large garlic cloves, unpeeled, woody ends trimmed

4 Tbsp [60 ml] extra-virgin olive oil, plus more for drizzling

Fine sea salt and freshly ground black pepper

⅓ cup [80 g] plain whole-milk yogurt

2 Tbsp tahini

1½ Tbsp pure maple syrup, preferably grade B, plus more as needed

1½ Tbsp freshly squeezed lemon juice

1 tsp harissa, plus more to taste

2 Tbsp salted roasted pumpkin seeds (pepitas)

Preheat the oven to 375°F [190°C].

Halve the pumpkin and use a spoon to scoop out the seeds and strings. Cut each half into four evenly sized wedges and put in a 9-by-13-in [23-by-33-cm] baking dish. Drop the garlic into the dish, drizzle everything with 2 Tbsp of the olive oil, and sprinkle with ½ tsp salt and ¼ tsp pepper. Toss to coat. Roast, flipping the pumpkin wedges after about 20 minutes, until a skewer inserted into the thickest piece of pumpkin meets no resistance, 40 to 50 minutes. Let cool completely in the baking dish.

Using a spoon, scoop the flesh from the pumpkin wedges, leaving only the skin behind, and put in a food processor. Remove the garlic cloves from the baking dish, peel, and add to the food processor, along with the yogurt, tahini, maple syrup, lemon juice, harissa, ½ tsp salt, and ¼ tsp pepper. Process to a smooth, thick purée, 1 to 1½ minutes, scraping down the bowl as needed. With the machine running, stream in the remaining 2 Tbsp olive oil and continue to process until the mixture is as smooth as it can be, about 1 minute, scraping down the bowl as needed. Taste and adjust the seasoning with more salt, pepper, maple syrup, and harissa, if needed.

CONTINUED

Transfer the dip to a wide, shallow bowl for serving. Cover and let stand at room temperature for about 30 minutes to allow the flavors to meld.

Use the back of a spoon to swirl the surface of the dip. Sprinkle with the pumpkin seeds, drizzle with olive oil, and serve.

NOTE / *Kabocha pumpkins vary in moisture content and sweetness. If you find that your dip is too thick after puréeing, stir in some water. Your dip may also require more maple syrup to balance the tang of the yogurt and the heat of the harissa.*

MAKES / about 2½ cups [580 g]

SERVE WITH / Crackers, crudités, lavash, pita bread, pita chips

STORAGE / Can be refrigerated without garnish for up to 5 days (flavor improves with storage); bring to room temperature, stir to recombine, and garnish before serving

ZUCCHINI AND SUNFLOWER SEED DIP

4½ lb [2 kg] zucchini (see Note)

½ cup [70 g] salted roasted sunflower seeds (see Note), plus more for garnish

2½ Tbsp freshly squeezed lemon juice

2 medium garlic cloves, germ removed (see page 9), chopped

⅛ tsp cayenne pepper, plus more for garnish

Fine sea salt and freshly ground black pepper

¼ cup [60 ml] extra-virgin olive oil, plus more for drizzling

Position an oven rack so that it is about 5 in [12 cm] from the broiler and preheat the broiler. Line a rimmed baking sheet with aluminum foil.

Arrange the zucchini on the prepared baking sheet. Broil the zucchini, using tongs to rotate them every 15 minutes, until blackened and charred all over, about 1 hour. Let cool on the baking sheet for 20 to 30 minutes.

Set a large fine-mesh strainer over a medium bowl. Using a paring knife, slit open each zucchini, and then use a spoon to scoop the pulp into the strainer; make sure to scrape off any pulp that clings to the skin. Let the pulp drain for about 30 minutes, stirring occasionally to release the moisture. Discard the liquid.

In a food processor, pulse the sunflower seeds until they form a paste that collects in small clumps, about 1½ minutes. Add the drained zucchini pulp, lemon juice, garlic, cayenne, 1 tsp salt, and ¼ tsp black pepper. Process to a smooth purée, about 1 minute, scraping down the bowl once or twice. With the machine running, stream in the olive oil and continue to process until the mixture is as smooth as it can be, about 1 minute, scraping down the bowl once or twice. Taste and adjust the seasoning with more salt and pepper, if needed.

Transfer the dip to a wide, shallow bowl for serving. Cover and let stand at room temperature for 1 hour to allow the flavors to meld.

Use the back of a spoon to swirl the surface of the dip. Sprinkle with sunflower seeds, dust with cayenne, drizzle with olive oil, and serve.

NOTES / *Zucchini vary greatly in size. Look for ones that weigh 10 to 12 oz [280 to 340 g] each, so they cook at the same rate.*

For a dip with a perfectly smooth and silky texture, use sunflower butter instead of sunflower seeds—but make sure to use unsweetened sunflower butter. Simply purée ⅓ cup [80 g] along with the zucchini pulp.

Creamy, bold, spicy, herbaceous

MAKES / about 2½ cups [620 g]

SERVE WITH / Corn chips, crackers, crudités, grissini, pita chips, toasted baguette slices

STORAGE / Best served right away, but can be refrigerated for up to 1 day (color will dull slightly with storage); bring to room temperature and stir to recombine before serving

AVOCADO-CHERMOULA DIP

CHERMOULA

1 cup [20 g] packed fresh flat-leaf parsley leaves

2¼ cups [25 g] packed fresh cilantro leaves

1 large garlic clove, germ removed (see page 9), chopped

3 Tbsp extra-virgin olive oil

1 Tbsp freshly squeezed lemon juice

1½ tsp paprika

1 tsp red pepper flakes

¾ tsp ground cumin

¼ tsp ground coriander

½ tsp fine sea salt

3 large ripe Hass avocados

1½ Tbsp freshly squeezed lemon juice

Fine sea salt and freshly ground black pepper

TO MAKE THE CHERMOULA / In a food processor, combine all of the ingredients and process until the herbs are finely chopped and the mixture is well combined, 45 to 60 seconds, scraping down the bowl once or twice. Set aside.

Halve the avocados and remove and discard the pits. Score the flesh with a dinner knife (cutting to, but not through, the skin) and scoop the flesh into a medium bowl. Add the lemon juice, ½ tsp salt, and ¼ tsp black pepper and use a dinner fork to mash the mixture to a rough purée. Add the chermoula and fold with a rubber spatula until the chermoula is evenly distributed. Taste and adjust the seasoning with more salt and pepper, if needed.

Press a sheet of plastic wrap directly against the surface of the dip to prevent discoloring and let stand at room temperature for about 30 minutes to allow the flavors to meld.

Transfer the dip to a wide, shallow bowl to serve.

OLIVES, NUTS & SEEDS

Chunky, tangy-sweet, subtly spicy, lightly citrusy

MAKES / about 1½ cups [330 g]

SERVE WITH / Fresh or toasted baguette slices

STORAGE / Can be refrigerated for up to 1 week; bring to room temperature and stir to recombine before serving

GREEN OLIVE AND RAISIN RELISH
WITH PINE NUTS

3 Tbsp pine nuts

1½ cups [225 g] pitted green olives (see Note), patted dry

½ cup [80 g] raisins

½ cup [10 g] loosely packed fresh flat-leaf parsley leaves

2 Tbsp extra-virgin olive oil

1½ Tbsp white wine vinegar

1½ Tbsp minced shallot

¼ tsp red pepper flakes

¼ tsp freshly ground black pepper

¼ tsp finely orange zest

Fine sea salt (optional)

In a small skillet over medium heat, toast the pine nuts, stirring frequently, until fragrant and golden, about 5 minutes. Let cool, and then coarsely chop. Set aside.

In a food processor, combine the olives, raisins, parsley, olive oil, vinegar, shallot, red pepper flakes, black pepper, and orange zest. Pulse about fifteen times, until the mixture is finely chopped, scraping the bowl down once or twice. Taste and adjust the seasoning with salt, if needed.

Transfer the relish to a wide, shallow bowl for serving and stir in the pine nuts. Cover and let stand at room temperature for about 1 hour to allow the flavors to meld before serving.

NOTE / *Good-quality imported green olives work best in this relish; canned green olives lack the brininess and punch needed for nicely balanced flavor.*

Rustic, intense, savory, briny, umami-rich

MAKES / about 1 cup [130 g]

SERVE WITH / Fresh or toasted baguette slices, pita bread

STORAGE / Can be refrigerated for up to 1 week; bring to room temperature and stir to recombine before serving

CLASSIC TAPENADE

2 cups [300 g] pitted kalamata olives, rinsed, drained, and patted dry

2 Tbsp capers, rinsed, drained, and patted dry

4 or 5 oil-packed anchovy fillets, rinsed, patted dry, and roughly chopped

1 medium garlic clove, germ removed (see page 9), minced to a paste

3 Tbsp extra-virgin olive oil

1 Tbsp freshly squeezed lemon juice

1½ tsp minced fresh thyme

In a food processor, combine all of the ingredients. Pulse about twelve times, until the mixture is finely chopped, scraping down the bowl once or twice. If you prefer a smoother texture, pulse a few more times.

Transfer the tapenade to a wide, shallow bowl for serving. Cover and let stand at room temperature for about 1 hour to allow the flavors to meld before serving.

MIXED OLIVE TAPENADE
WITH ARTICHOKES AND PRESERVED LEMON

One 14-oz [400-g] can artichoke hearts, drained, patted dry, and cut into rough ¾-in [2-cm] chunks

1½ cups [225 g] pitted mixed olives, patted dry

2 Tbsp capers, rinsed, drained, and patted dry

3 or 4 oil-packed anchovy fillets, rinsed, patted dry, and roughly chopped

2 medium garlic cloves, germ removed (see page 9), minced to a paste

3 Tbsp extra-virgin olive oil

1 Tbsp minced preserved lemon (see Note)

2 tsp minced fresh oregano

2 tsp freshly squeezed lemon juice

½ tsp freshly ground black pepper

Fresh basil leaves for garnish

In a food processor, combine all of the ingredients. Pulse fifteen to twenty times, until the mixture is finely chopped, scraping the bowl once or twice. If you prefer a smoother texture, pulse a few more times.

Transfer the tapenade to a wide, shallow bowl for serving. Cover and let stand at room temperature for about 1 hour to allow the flavors to meld.

Garnish with the basil leaves and serve.

NOTE / *Preserved lemons—lemons cured in salt—are a staple in Moroccan cuisine. They're often sold in well-stocked supermarkets, specialty food stores, and Middle Eastern grocery stores. If you're unable to find them, use ¾ tsp finely grated lemon zest instead.*

MAKES / about 1½ cups [330 g]

SERVE WITH / Crudités, roasted potatoes

STORAGE / Best served within a couple hours of making (with longer storage, the color dulls slightly and the garlic flavor loses its freshness)

WALNUT-GARLIC DIP
WITH SPINACH

1 cup [110 g] walnuts

1½ cups [40 g] cubed stale white bread trimmed of crust (½-in [12-mm] cubes; see Note)

Fine sea salt and freshly ground black pepper

2 medium garlic cloves, germ removed (see page 9), chopped

2 Tbsp water, plus more as needed

3 Tbsp freshly squeezed lemon juice, plus more as needed

1½ cups [30 g] loosely packed baby spinach

¼ cup plus 2 Tbsp [90 ml] extra-virgin olive oil

In a medium skillet over medium heat, toast the walnuts, stirring frequently, until fragrant and golden, 6 to 8 minutes. Let cool completely. Set aside 1 Tbsp for garnish. In a food processor, combine the remaining walnuts, the bread cubes, ½ tsp salt, and ½ tsp pepper. Process until the mixture is finely ground, 30 to 45 seconds. Add the garlic, water, and lemon juice and process to a thick, relatively smooth paste, 15 to 20 seconds. Add the spinach and process until combined, about 10 seconds. Scrape down the bowl as needed. With the machine running, stream in the olive oil. The dip should be creamy like yogurt, but not as thick as Greek yogurt. If it is too thick, scrape down the bowl and, with the machine running, stream in additional water, 1 tsp at a time. Taste and adjust the seasoning with more salt, pepper, and lemon juice, if needed.

Transfer the dip to a wide, shallow bowl for serving. Cover and let stand at room temperature for about 30 minutes to allow the flavors to meld.

Chop the reserved walnuts, sprinkle them over the top, and serve.

NOTE / *To stale fresh bread, lay the slices on a wire rack and leave at room temperature for about 4 hours. Alternatively, give them a couple of passes on the lowest setting of a toaster until the surface of the bread is dry but not browned.*

Intense, thick, nutty, sweet, spicy

MAKES / about 2 cups [480 g]

SERVE WITH / Corn chips, crudités, pita chips, toasted baguette slices

STORAGE / Can be refrigerated without garnish for up to 5 days; bring to room temperature, stir to recombine, and garnish before serving

PUMPKIN SEED DIP
WITH ROASTED TOMATOES AND SERRANO CHILE

1½ lb [680 g] plum tomatoes, cored, quartered lengthwise, and seeded

1 large serrano chile, stemmed, halved lengthwise, seeded, and ribs removed

1 Tbsp extra-virgin olive oil

Fine sea salt

3 large garlic cloves, unpeeled, woody ends trimmed

1¼ cups [140 g] salted roasted pumpkin seeds (pepitas)

2 Tbsp freshly squeezed lemon juice

½ cup [25 g] thinly sliced green onions (white and green parts), plus 2 Tbsp (green part only)

½ tsp ground cumin

Preheat the oven to 450°F [230°C]. Line a rimmed baking sheet with aluminum foil.

Combine the tomato quarters and chile halves in a large bowl. Drizzle with the olive oil, sprinkle with ¼ tsp salt, and toss to combine. Empty the bowl's contents onto the prepared baking sheet. Turn the tomatoes skin-side down and the chile halves skin-side up, distributing the tomatoes and chile in an even layer. Toss the garlic onto the baking sheet. Roast for 15 minutes. Remove the garlic cloves and set aside. Continue roasting the tomatoes and chile until the tomatoes have softened and the chile skin has charred, about 15 minutes more. Let cool on the baking sheet.

In a food processor, process the pumpkin seeds and lemon juice until the seeds are finely ground, about 1 minute, scraping down the bowl once or twice. Peel the garlic cloves and drop them into the food processor. Add the roasted tomatoes and chile, ½ cup [25 g] green onions, cumin, and ½ tsp salt. Process until the mixture is as smooth as it can be, 1 to 1½ minutes, scraping down the bowl as needed. Taste and adjust the seasoning with more salt if needed.

Transfer the dip to a wide, shallow bowl for serving. Cover and let stand at room temperature for about 30 minutes to allow the flavors to meld.

Sprinkle with the 2 Tbsp green onions and serve.

MAKES / about ½ cup [50 g]

SERVE WITH / Fresh baguette slices, focaccia, pita bread

STORAGE / Can be refrigerated for up to 2 days; bring to room temperature before serving

ZA'ATAR
WITH FRESH THYME

3 Tbsp sesame seeds

½ tsp dried oregano

3 Tbsp minced fresh thyme

2 tsp ground sumac

¾ tsp kosher salt

¼ tsp freshly ground black pepper

Extra-virgin olive oil for serving

In a small skillet over medium heat, toast the sesame seeds, stirring frequently, until fragrant and a shade darker in color, about 3 minutes. Transfer to a small bowl and let cool completely.

Put the sesame seeds and dried oregano in an electric spice grinder or a coffee grinder and pulse three or four times, until the seeds are broken apart. Transfer to a small shallow bowl and add the thyme, sumac, salt, and pepper. Stir until well combined.

Transfer the za'atar to a wide, shallow bowl for serving. Offer olive oil in a small dish alongside. Dip pieces of bread in the olive oil and then dip into the za'atar or sprinkle za'atar over the top. Alternatively, pour 2 to 3 Tbsp olive oil into a small dish and stir in almost an equal amount of za'atar; dip bread into this mixture, making sure to scoop up some za'atar with each dunk.

Fragrant, nutty, spicy, savory, earthy, pungent

MAKES / about 1 cup [130 g]

SERVE WITH / Fresh baguette slices, focaccia, pita bread

STORAGE / Can be stored in an airtight container at room temperature for up to 2 weeks

PISTACHIO DUKKAH

½ cup [60 g] shelled
unsalted roasted pistachios

2½ Tbsp coriander seeds

2 Tbsp cumin seeds

1 tsp fennel seeds

¼ cup [35 g] sesame seeds

1½ tsp freshly ground
black pepper

1 tsp dried mint

1 tsp kosher salt

Extra-virgin olive oil for
serving

In a medium skillet over medium heat, toast the pistachios, stirring frequently, until fragrant, about 7 minutes. Transfer to a food processor and let cool.

In the same skillet over medium heat, toast the coriander seeds, cumin seeds, and fennel seeds, stirring frequently, until fragrant, about 3 minutes. Transfer to a small bowl and let cool.

Put the sesame seeds in the skillet and toast over medium heat, stirring frequently, until fragrant and a shade darker in color, about 3 minutes. Transfer to a second small bowl and let cool.

When everything has cooled, pulse the pistachios about fifteen times, until coarsely chopped. Add the whole spices, the black pepper, and dried mint and pulse another fifteen times, until evenly ground (don't overprocess, which will cause the mixture to become pasty). Add the sesame seeds and salt and pulse two or three times, just until the sesame seeds are broken up.

Transfer the dukkah to a small, shallow bowl for serving. Offer olive oil in a small dish alongside. Dip pieces of bread in the olive oil and then dip into the dukkah or sprinkle dukkah over the top.

YOGURT
&
CHEESE

Thick, creamy, tangy, fresh, herbaceous

MAKES / about 1⅔ cups [500 g]

SERVE WITH / Crackers, pita chips, toasted baguette slices

STORAGE / Can be refrigerated without garnish for up to 2 days; bring to room temperature, stir to recombine, and garnish before serving

HERBED LABNEH
WITH GARLIC OIL AND TOMATOES

GARLIC OIL

½ cup [120 ml] extra-virgin olive oil

5 medium garlic cloves, thinly sliced

Labneh (see page 86)

2 green onions (white and green parts), thinly sliced

1½ Tbsp chopped fresh mint

1½ Tbsp chopped fresh flat-leaf parsley

1 Tbsp chopped fresh dill

⅛ tsp finely grated lemon zest, plus 2 tsp freshly squeezed lemon juice

Fine sea salt and freshly ground black pepper

⅓ cup [50 g] grape tomatoes

TO MAKE THE GARLIC OIL / In a small saucepan, combine the olive oil and garlic. Set the pan over medium heat and gently cook the mixture, swirling occasionally, until the garlic has lightened in color and no longer smells raw, 5 to 6 minutes; the oil should bubble lazily (adjust the heat as needed so that the garlic doesn't scorch). Transfer the mixture to a heatproof jar and refrigerate for up to 2 weeks.

Pour 1½ Tbsp of the cooled oil (leaving the garlic slices behind) into a medium bowl. Add the labneh, green onions, mint, parsley, dill, lemon zest, lemon juice, ¾ tsp salt, and ¼ tsp pepper and stir to combine. Taste and adjust the seasoning with more salt and pepper, if needed. Set aside.

Cut each tomato lengthwise into quarters. Sprinkle the tomatoes with a big pinch of salt and a few grinds of pepper and toss to combine.

Transfer the labneh to a wide, shallow bowl for serving.

Use the back of a spoon to swirl the surface of the labneh. Top with the tomatoes, drizzle with 1 to 2 Tbsp garlic oil, and serve.

NOTE / *Bring garlic oil to room temperature before use in dressings or as dipping oil for bread. If you prefer, you can substitute good-quality store-bought garlic-infused olive oil.*

Thick, creamy, tangy, refreshing

MAKES / about 1½ cups [390 g]

SERVE WITH / Crudités, pita chips

STORAGE / Can be refrigerated without garnish for up to 5 days; bring to cool room temperature, stir to recombine, and garnish before serving

LABNEH
WITH OLIVE OIL AND ZA'ATAR

LABNEH

2 cups [480 g] whole-milk Greek yogurt

¼ tsp fine sea salt

2 Tbsp Za'atar with Fresh Thyme (page 79)

Extra-virgin olive oil for drizzling

TO MAKE THE LABNEH / Line a large fine-mesh strainer with a double layer of cheesecloth, leaving about 2 in [5 cm] of overhang. Set the strainer over a bowl.

In a small bowl, stir together the yogurt and salt. Transfer the yogurt to the prepared strainer and cover the surface with the overhanging ends of cheesecloth. Refrigerate for 24 hours.

Transfer the labneh to a wide, shallow bowl for serving. Cover and let stand at room temperature for about 30 minutes to allow it to lose its chill.

Use the back of a spoon to swirl the surface of the labneh. Sprinkle with the za'atar, drizzle with olive oil, and serve.

Creamy, tangy, cooling, fresh

MAKES / about 2⅓ cups [565 g]

SERVE WITH / Crackers, pita bread, pita chips

STORAGE / Best served the day it's made, but can be refrigerated without garnish for up to 1 day; bring to room temperature, stir to recombine, and garnish before serving

CUCUMBER TZATZIKI

1 large cucumber, peeled, seeded, and grated on the large holes of a box grater

Fine sea salt

1½ cups [360 g] whole-milk Greek yogurt

1 Tbsp finely chopped fresh mint

1 Tbsp finely chopped fresh dill

2 small garlic cloves, germ removed (see page 9), minced to a paste

1 Tbsp freshly squeezed lemon juice

1 Tbsp extra-virgin olive oil, plus more for drizzling

Freshly ground black pepper

Put the grated cucumber in a large fine-mesh strainer set over a bowl, sprinkle with ¼ tsp salt, and toss well. Let the cucumber drain for 30 minutes.

Press down on the cucumber to extract more liquid. Transfer to a clean medium bowl and discard the liquid. Add the yogurt, mint, dill, garlic, lemon juice, olive oil, ¾ tsp salt, and ½ tsp pepper and stir to combine. Taste and adjust the seasoning with more salt and pepper, if needed.

Transfer the tzatziki to a wide, shallow bowl for serving. Cover and let stand at room temperature for 30 minutes to allow the flavors to meld.

Use the back of a spoon to swirl the surface of the dip. Drizzle with olive oil and serve.

MAKES / about 2½ cups [860 g]

SERVE WITH / Crackers, pita bread, pita chips

STORAGE / Best served the day it's made, but can be refrigerated without garnish for up to 2 days; bring to room temperature, stir to recombine, and garnish before serving.

GOLDEN BEET TZATZIKI

12 oz [340 g] golden beets (without greens), scrubbed (see Note)

1½ cups [360 g] whole-milk Greek yogurt

1½ Tbsp finely chopped fresh dill, plus more for garnish

1 medium garlic clove, germ removed (see page 9), minced to a paste

½ tsp finely grated lemon zest, plus 1 Tbsp freshly squeezed lemon juice

1 Tbsp extra-virgin olive oil, plus more for drizzling

Fine sea salt and freshly ground black pepper

Preheat the oven to 350°F [180°C].

Put the beets in a small baking dish. Add the ¼ cup [60 ml] water and cover tightly with foil. Roast until a metal skewer inserted into the largest beet meets absolutely no resistance, 1 to 1½ hours, depending on the size of the beets. Uncover and let cool to room temperature.

Slip the skins off the beets, using a paring knife to scrape off any areas that cling. Grate the beets on the large holes of a box grater.

In a medium bowl, combine the grated beets, yogurt, dill, garlic, lemon zest, lemon juice, olive oil, ¾ tsp salt, and ½ tsp pepper and stir well. Taste and adjust the seasoning with more salt and pepper, if needed.

Transfer the tzatziki to a wide, shallow bowl for serving. Cover and let stand at room temperature for about 30 minutes to allow the flavors to meld.

Use the back of a spoon to swirl the surface of the dip. Drizzle with olive oil, sprinkle with dill, and serve.

NOTE / *You can substitute red beets for the golden beets. They will give the tzatziki a vibrant fuschia color and a deeper, earthier flavor.*

Creamy, savory-sweet, tangy, slightly spicy, a touch citrusy

MAKES / about 1⅔ cups [450 g]

SERVE WITH / Crackers, toasted baguette slices

STORAGE / Best served right away, but can be refrigerated without garnish for up to 3 days; bring to room temperature before serving

WHIPPED GOAT CHEESE
WITH WALNUTS AND CHILE-HONEY DRIZZLE

⅓ cup [35 g] chopped walnuts

3 Tbsp honey

½ tsp good-quality red pepper flakes, preferably Aleppo pepper or *piment d'Espelette* (see Note)

8 oz [230 g] goat cheese, crumbled

½ cup [120 g] Greek-style yogurt

½ tsp finely grated lemon zest

In a small skillet over medium heat, toast the walnuts, stirring frequently, until fragrant and golden, 6 to 8 minutes. Let cool completely.

In a small saucepan over medium heat, warm the honey and red pepper flakes until barely simmering. Remove from the heat and let cool completely.

In a the bowl of a stand mixer fitted with the whisk attachment or with a handheld mixer, whip the goat cheese, yogurt, and lemon zest on medium-high speed until the mixture is smooth and creamy, about 2 minutes, scraping down the bowl as needed. Using a rubber spatula, fold in the toasted walnuts.

Transfer the goat cheese to a wide, shallow bowl for serving, spreading it to the edges.

Use the back of a spoon to swirl the surface of the dip. Drizzle with the honey mixture, allowing it to pool on the surface. (If the honey is too viscous to drizzle easily, thin it with water, adding only ⅛ tsp at a time.) Serve right away.

NOTE / *Seed-free and very flavorful—though not incendiary— red pepper flakes work best in this recipe. Aleppo pepper from Turkey and* piment d'Espelette *from the Basque region are two good options. If only standard red pepper flakes are available, reduce the amount to ¼ to ⅜ tsp.*

Lush, savory-sweet, slightly tangy, nutty, subtly herbaceous

MAKES / about 1½ cups [430 g]

SERVE WITH / Crackers, toasted baguette slices

STORAGE / Best served within a couple hours of making (while the nuts are crunchy), but can be refrigerated without garnish for up to 3 days; bring to room temperature, stir to recombine, and garnish before serving

GOAT CHEESE AND DATE SPREAD
WITH HAZELNUTS AND THYME

½ cup [60 g] hazelnuts (see Note)

8 oz [230 g] goat cheese, crumbled, at room temperature

¼ cup [60 g] whole-milk Greek yogurt

4 oz [115 g] moist, plump dates, pitted and finely chopped

1 tsp minced fresh thyme, plus more for garnish

¼ tsp finely grated lemon zest

Fine sea salt and freshly ground black pepper

In a small skillet over medium heat, toast the hazelnuts, stirring frequently, until fragrant, 6 to 8 minutes. Let cool, then rub the nuts in a clean kitchen towel to remove the skins (some skins will remain—this is fine). Coarsely chop the nuts and reserve a heaping 1 Tbsp for garnish.

In a medium bowl, combined the goat cheese and yogurt and mix with a rubber spatula until well blended. Add the remaining hazelnuts, the dates, thyme, lemon zest, a big pinch of salt, and a few grinds of pepper and mix, mashing the mixture with the spatula until thoroughly combined. Taste and adjust the seasoning with more salt and pepper, if needed.

Transfer the spread to a wide, shallow bowl for serving. Cover and let stand at room temperature for about 30 minutes to allow the flavors to meld.

Sprinkle with the reserved hazelnuts and some minced thyme and serve.

NOTE / *Many grocery stores now sell hazelnuts that are already toasted (or roasted) and skinned. If you can find them, use them instead of toasting and skinning your own.*

MAKES / about 1½ cups [340 g]

SERVE WITH / Crackers, crudités, toasted baguette slices

STORAGE / Can be refrigerated without garnish for up to 3 days; bring to room temperature, stir to recombine, and garnish before serving

FETA SPREAD
WITH GREEN OLIVES AND SUN-DRIED TOMATOES

8 oz [230 g] feta cheese, crumbled

2 Tbsp extra-virgin olive oil

1½ Tbsp freshly squeezed lemon juice

1 small garlic clove, germ removed (see page 9), chopped

¼ tsp red pepper flakes

⅓ cup [50 g] oil-packed sun-dried tomatoes, rinsed, drained, and finely chopped

¼ cup [30 g] finely chopped pitted green olives, rinsed, drained, and patted dry

¼ cup [10 g] thinly sliced green onions (white and green parts), plus 2 Tbsp (green part only)

In a food processor, combine the feta, olive oil, lemon juice, garlic, and red pepper flakes. Process until the feta is smooth, 30 to 45 seconds, scraping down the bowl once or twice. Transfer the feta to a medium bowl and stir in the sun-dried tomatoes, olives, and ¼ cup [10 g] green onions.

Transfer the spread to a wide, shallow bowl for serving. Cover and let stand at room temperature for about 30 minutes to allow the flavors to meld.

Garnish with the remaining 2 Tbsp green onions and serve.

MAKES / about 2½ cups [570 g]

SERVE WITH / Crudités, pita bread, pita chips, toasted baguette slices

STORAGE / Can be refrigerated without garnish for up to 5 days; garnish before serving

ROASTED RED PEPPER AND CHIPOTLE WHIPPED FETA

12 oz [340 g] feta cheese, crumbled

½ cup [100 g] drained jarred roasted red peppers, patted dry

3 Tbsp extra-virgin olive oil

1 tsp minced seeded chipotle chile in adobo, plus 2 tsp adobo sauce

2 tsp freshly squeezed lemon juice

½ tsp freshly ground black pepper

Sliced green onions (green part only) for garnish

Paprika or smoked paprika for garnish

In a food processor, combine the feta, red peppers, olive oil, minced chipotle, adobo sauce, lemon juice, and black pepper. Process until the mixture is as smooth as it can be, 45 to 60 seconds, scraping down the bowl once or twice. The dip will be very fluid at this point.

Transfer to an airtight container and refrigerate for about 2 hours to allow the flavors to meld and the consistency to set up.

Transfer the feta to a wide, shallow bowl for serving. Let stand at room temperature for about 15 minutes, then stir to recombine.

Garnish with sliced green onions, sprinkle with paprika, and serve.

Creamy, sweet-savory, citrusy, a touch floral

MAKES / about 2 cups [460 g]

SERVE WITH / Crackers, toasted baguette slices

STORAGE / Best served the day it's made, but can be refrigerated without garnish for up to 3 days; bring to room temperature, stir to recombine, and garnish before serving

RICOTTA AND SHERRIED FIGS
WITH ORANGE AND ROSEMARY

1½ cups [360 g] whole-milk ricotta cheese

3 oz [85 g] dried Mission figs, stemmed and finely diced

¼ cup plus 2 Tbsp [90 ml] amontillado sherry

2 Tbsp honey

1 tsp minced fresh rosemary

⅝ tsp fine sea salt

¼ tsp finely grated orange zest

2 Tbsp sliced almonds

Line a large fine-mesh strainer with a double layer of cheesecloth, leaving about 2 in [5 cm] of overhang. Set the strainer over a bowl. Put the ricotta in the prepared strainer and cover the surface with the overhanging cheesecloth. Refrigerate overnight.

Put the figs in a small heatproof bowl. In a small saucepan, bring the sherry to a simmer over medium heat and then pour over the figs. Stir to moisten all the figs. Cover and let soak overnight at room temperature.

The next day, drain the figs in a fine-mesh strainer and pat them dry with paper towels. Reserve 2 Tbsp of figs for garnish. In a medium bowl, combine the remaining figs, drained ricotta, honey, rosemary, salt, and orange zest and stir until well blended.

Transfer the ricotta to a wide, shallow bowl for serving. Cover and let stand at room temperature for about 30 minutes to allow the flavors to meld.

In a small skillet over medium heat, toast the almonds, stirring frequently, until golden and fragrant, 6 to 8 minutes. Let cool completely.

Sprinkle the ricotta with the toasted almonds, top with the reserved figs, and serve.

SALT
&
SEA

Rustic, meaty, concentrated, umami-rich, subtly sweet, smoky

MAKES / about 2¼ cups [510 g]

SERVE WITH / Crackers, fresh or toasted baguette slices

STORAGE / Can be refrigerated without garnish for up to 3 days; bring to room temperature, stir to recombine, and garnish before serving

SARDINE PÂTÉ
WITH SWEET PEPPERS AND SUN-DRIED TOMATOES

1½ Tbsp extra-virgin olive oil

1 large shallot, minced

¼ cup [35 g] finely chopped drained oil-packed sun-dried tomatoes

1 medium garlic clove, minced

1½ tsp paprika

⅛ tsp cayenne pepper

Three 3¾-oz [106-g] cans smoked sardines in olive oil, drained well (see Note)

3 Tbsp unsalted butter, at room temperature

¾ tsp fine sea salt

¼ tsp ground black pepper

2½ Tbsp freshly squeezed lemon juice

½ cup [100 g] drained jarred roasted red peppers, patted dry and finely chopped, plus 1 Tbsp

3 Tbsp chopped fresh flat-leaf parsley, plus more for garnish

In a small skillet over medium heat, warm the olive oil. Add the shallot and cook, stirring frequently, until softened, about 3 minutes. Turn the heat to medium-low and add the sun-dried tomatoes, garlic, paprika, and cayenne and cook, stirring constantly, until the garlic no longer smells raw, about 2 minutes. Transfer to a small bowl and let cool completely.

In a medium bowl, combine the sardines, butter, salt, and black pepper and mash with a fork or wooden spoon until the sardines are broken down and the mixture is well combined. Stir in the cooled shallot mixture, the lemon juice, roasted red peppers, and parsley.

Transfer the pâté to a wide, shallow bowl for serving. Cover and let stand at room temperature for about 30 minutes to allow the flavors to meld.

Garnish with the remaining 1 Tbsp roasted red pepper and parsley and serve.

NOTE / *If you prefer, use regular (not smoked) sardines in this spread. Or for a more subtle smoky flavor, use a combination of regular and smoked sardines.*

MAKES / about 1¼ cups [260 g]

SERVE WITH / Crudités (vegetables with textures that can grip or shapes that can scoop work particularly well), fresh baguette slices, roasted potatoes

STORAGE / Best served right away

WARM GARLIC, ANCHOVY, AND OLIVE OIL DIP
(BAGNA CAUDA)

¾ cup [180 ml] extra-virgin olive oil

4 Tbsp [55 g] unsalted butter, cut into 4 pieces

8 to 10 medium garlic cloves, minced

10 to 12 oil-packed anchovy fillets, rinsed, patted dry, and minced

Fine sea salt and freshly ground black pepper

⅛ tsp finely grated lemon zest (optional)

Warm a wide, shallow serving bowl by filling it with simmering water. Set it aside while you make the dip.

In a small saucepan, combine the olive oil, butter, garlic, and anchovies. Set the pan over medium heat and cook, stirring frequently, until the butter has melted, the anchovies have broken down, and the garlic has softened and is no longer raw, 5 to 6 minutes. The mixture should bubble steadily but gently and may foam up on the surface; adjust the heat as needed and watch carefully so that the garlic does not scorch. Season with salt (the dip may need only a pinch) and pepper, and then stir in the lemon zest (if using).

Cover the saucepan and set it aside, off the heat. (If you're not ready to serve the dip, it will hold this way for up to 1 hour. Just before serving, rewarm gently over low heat, and make sure your serving bowl is warm, too.) Empty the hot water out of the serving bowl and wipe the bowl dry.

Transfer the dip to the prepared bowl, making sure to scrape out the anchovy and garlic bits in the bottom of the pan.

Serve warm, ideally with a spoon for scooping up the bits. (If the dip cools to room temperature on the table, don't fret—it may not be as aromatic as when hot, but it will keep its fluid consistency.)

Rich, creamy, savory, meaty, intense, umami-packed

MAKES / about 1⅔ cups [360 g]

SERVE WITH / Crudités, grissini, pita chips, toasted baguette slices

STORAGE / Can be refrigerated without garnish for up to 2 days (the green onion will dull slightly in color); bring to room temperature, stir to recombine, and garnish before serving

TUNA DIP
WITH CAPERS, GREEN ONIONS, AND LEMON

Two 5-oz [142-g] cans tuna in olive oil, drained well

4 Tbsp [55 g] unsalted butter, cut into small pieces, at room temperature

3 Tbsp capers, rinsed, drained, and patted dry

1½ tsp finely grated lemon zest, plus 2 Tbsp freshly squeezed lemon juice

6 Tbsp [20 g] thinly sliced green onions (white and green parts), plus 2 Tbsp (green part only)

Pinch of cayenne pepper

Fine sea salt and freshly ground black pepper

2 Tbsp extra-virgin olive oil, plus more as needed

In a food processor, combine the tuna, butter, capers, lemon zest, lemon juice, 6 Tbsp [20 g] green onions, cayenne, ½ tsp salt, and ¼ tsp pepper. Process to a thick, relatively smooth purée, about 45 seconds, scraping down the bowl as needed. With the machine running, stream in the olive oil and process until the mixture is as smooth as it can be, 45 to 60 seconds, scraping down the bowl once or twice. Check the consistency of the dip—it should be creamy and soft, but able to hold its shape on a spoon. If it's stiff and dry, stream in up to an additional 2 Tbsp olive oil. Taste and adjust the seasoning with more salt and pepper, if needed.

Transfer the dip to a wide, shallow bowl for serving. Cover and let stand at room temperature for about 30 minutes to allow the flavors to meld.

Garnish with the remaining 2 Tbsp green onions and a few grinds of pepper and serve.

Rustic, savory, meaty, intense, briny, slightly spicy

MAKES / about 2¼ cups [430 g]

SERVE WITH / Crackers, fresh or toasted baguette slices

STORAGE / Can be refrigerated without garnish for up to 3 days; bring to room temperature, stir to recombine, and garnish before serving

TUNA OLIVADE
WITH SWEET PEPPERS AND FENNEL SEED

1 cup [150 g] pitted kalamata olives, rinsed, drained, and patted dry

½ cup [100 g] drained jarred roasted red bell peppers, patted dry and chopped

3 Tbsp chopped seeded pepperoncini

2 Tbsp extra-virgin olive oil

1½ tsp freshly squeezed lemon juice

1 or 2 oil-packed anchovy fillets, rinsed, patted dry, and roughly chopped

1 medium garlic clove, germ removed (see page 9), chopped

½ tsp chopped fresh thyme

½ tsp fennel seeds

¼ tsp red pepper flakes

One 5-oz [142-g] can tuna in olive oil, drained well and finely flaked

3 Tbsp chopped fresh flat-leaf parsley, plus torn leaves for garnish

In a food processor, combine the olives, red peppers, pepperoncini, olive oil, lemon juice, anchovies, garlic, thyme, fennel seeds, and red pepper flakes. Pulse ten to twelve times, until the mixture is finely chopped, scraping down the bowl once or twice.

Transfer the mixture to a medium bowl and add the tuna and parsley, stirring until well combined.

Transfer the olivade to a wide, shallow bowl for serving. Cover and let stand at room temperature for about 30 minutes to allow the flavors to meld.

Garnish with parsley and serve.

Rich, savory, super-smoky, fishy (in a good way)

MAKES / about 3½ cups [790 g]

SERVE WITH / Crudités, toasted baguette slices

STORAGE / Best served right away, but can be assembled and refrigerated in the baking dish for up to 2 hours; let stand at room temperature for 30 minutes and then sprinkle with the Parmigiano just before baking.

SMOKED TROUT BRANDADE

1 lb [455 g] russet potatoes, scrubbed

1 cup [240 ml] half-and-half

2 medium garlic cloves, peeled and crushed

1 dried bay leaf

One 8-oz [230-g] package smoked trout fillets

½ cup [120 ml] mild extra-virgin olive oil

2 tsp freshly squeezed lemon juice

Fine sea salt and freshly ground black pepper

3 Tbsp grated Parmigiano-Reggiano cheese

Put the potatoes in a medium saucepan and cover with about 1 in [2.5 cm] water. Bring to a boil over high heat, then lower the heat to maintain a lively simmer. Cover partially and simmer, adjusting the heat as needed, until a skewer inserted into the largest potato meets no resistance, 25 to 30 minutes.

While the potatoes cook, in a small saucepan, bring the half-and-half, garlic, and bay leaf to a simmer over medium heat. Simmer, partially covered, until the garlic has softened, 6 to 8 minutes. Cover the pan and set aside off the heat to allow the garlic and bay leaf to infuse the half-and-half.

Preheat the oven to 425°F [220°C]. Lightly oil a shallow, broiler-safe 4-cup [960-ml] baking dish or gratin dish.

Peel off and discard the skins from the trout fillets. Break the flesh into fine flakes and set aside.

CONTINUED

When the potatoes are ready, drain them and set aside for a few minutes to cool. Remove the skins (if you like, protect your hands with a kitchen towel or potholder). Spoon the garlic cloves out of the half-and half. While the potatoes are still hot, put them, along with the garlic cloves, through a potato ricer and back into the saucepan or into a medium bowl. Stir the olive oil into the hot riced potatoes until combined. Discard the bay leaf from the half-and-half and stir the half-and-half into the potato mixture. (It will be very soupy at this point but will thicken once you add the fish.) Add the trout, lemon juice, a pinch of salt, and ¼ tsp pepper. Fold until the mixture is well combined. Taste and adjust the seasoning with more salt and pepper, if needed.

Transfer the mixture to the prepared baking dish and spread into an even layer. Sprinkle with the Parmigiano. Bake the brandade until heated through, 15 to 20 minutes. Turn on the broiler and broil until the surface is lightly browned, 2 to 3 minutes. Let cool for 5 minutes.

Serve warm.

ACKNOWLEDGMENTS

It takes a village to make even a small book like this one. I would like to thank the incredibly talented people at Chronicle Books, especially Lorena Jones, Alice Chau, Doug Ogan, Tera Killip, Steve Kim, and Laura Rothman for their help in creating this handsome little volume.

Photographer Angie Cao and food stylist Fanny Pan made humble dips and spreads look more eye-catching and elegant than I thought possible. I am so appreciative of their hard work and amazing aesthetic.

I owe an enormous debt of gratitude to Adam Ried, who, as my dip counselor and good friend, made himself available for phone and IM consultations in the wee hours of the night (well, morning, actually). A canned-fish afishionado (groan—bad joke), he's responsible for introducing me to my newest addiction: sardine pâté.

I send out a giant thank-you to Sandra Wu for expertly testing recipes at a moment's notice. How lucky I am that our paths crossed at *Cook's Illustrated*.

Friends and neighbors Shaul Teplinsky and Joe Hao and Riccardo and Tracy Turchetto were always willing to lend their palates and fridge space. Thanks to them for being game, and for suffering multiple versions of multiple dips.

I owe so much to my mom, whose support has been unwavering, even when I decided to go to culinary school after finishing college and then dropping out of design school. Her great cooking and appreciation of good food sent me down this path.

Finally, I'd like to thank Christyan Mitchell, my sounding board, supertaster, kimchee pancake maker, occasional dish dryer, and much better half, for putting up with me for all these years. Here's to many more, always in the company of French bulldogs.

INDEX